Dave Harley

Mindfulness in a Digital World

palgrave
macmillan

Palgrave Studies in Cyberpsychology

Series Editor
Jens Binder, Nottingham Trent University, Nottingham, UK

Palgrave Studies in Cyberpsychology aims to foster and to chart the scope of research driven by a psychological understanding of the effects of the 'new technology' that is shaping our world after the digital revolution. The series takes an inclusive approach and considers all aspects of human behaviours and experiential states in relation to digital technologies, to the Internet, and to virtual environments. As such, Cyberpsychology reaches out to several neighbouring disciplines, from Human-Computer Interaction to Media and Communication Studies. A core question underpinning the series concerns the actual psychological novelty of new technology. To what extent do we need to expand conventional theories and models to account for cyberpsychological phenomena? At which points is the ubiquitous digitisation of our everyday lives shifting the focus of research questions and research needs? Where do we see implications for our psychological functioning that are likely to outlast shortlived fashions in technology use?

Dave Harley
School of Humanities and Social Science
University of Brighton
Brighton, UK

Palgrave Studies in Cyberpsychology
ISBN 978-3-031-19406-1   ISBN 978-3-031-19407-8 (eBook)
https://doi.org/10.1007/978-3-031-19407-8

© The Editor(s) (if applicable) and The Author(s), under exclusive license to Springer Nature Switzerland AG 2022
This work is subject to copyright. All rights are solely and exclusively licensed by the Publisher, whether the whole or part of the material is concerned, specifically the rights of translation, reprinting, reuse of illustrations, recitation, broadcasting, reproduction on microfilms or in any other physical way, and transmission or information storage and retrieval, electronic adaptation, computer software, or by similar or dissimilar methodology now known or hereafter developed.
The use of general descriptive names, registered names, trademarks, service marks, etc. in this publication does not imply, even in the absence of a specific statement, that such names are exempt from the relevant protective laws and regulations and therefore free for general use.
The publisher, the authors, and the editors are safe to assume that the advice and information in this book are believed to be true and accurate at the date of publication. Neither the publisher nor the authors or the editors give a warranty, expressed or implied, with respect to the material contained herein or for any errors or omissions that may have been made. The publisher remains neutral with regard to jurisdictional claims in published maps and institutional affiliations.

This Palgrave Macmillan imprint is published by the registered company Springer Nature Switzerland AG
The registered company address is: Gewerbestrasse 11, 6330 Cham, Switzerland

For Gonzo and Robin

Preface

Human beings have known for millennia that simply being in the present moment is a skill that has immediate and long-lasting benefits. My first encounter with this philosophy as a way of living came in 1990 when I learned to meditate at the Brighton Buddhist Centre whilst studying for my Psychology undergraduate degree. At the same time, I started to consume the writings of non-dualist philosophers such as Jiddu Krishnamurti and Douglas Harding who helped me to understand the limitations of the Western view of the self. I later became involved in mindfulness practise as another route into this non-dual experience of being. This way of approaching life proved to be an invaluable discovery for my inner life but strangely never connected in any meaningful way with my psychological research.

1990 was also the year that I first encountered a networked computer, signalling the emergence of another societal and technological transformation that was emerging at that time, i.e. that of the internet revolution. Over the intervening 30 years, digital technology has transformed the way that we live and has come to dominate our experience of everyday life. My psychological research since then has focused on making sense of the relationships that we develop with digital technologies, looking at how we integrate them into our lives, how they shape the way that we think about the world and our understanding of ourselves. This research has been primarily with older people and university students. What has become apparent throughout all this research is just how close and intimate our minds have become with digital technologies, almost as if they were acting as cognitive prostheses, creating potential for personal and social transformation but also introducing new psychological dilemmas that we find difficult to recognise let alone address. It is clear that social media, for instance, can transform social opportunities whatever your age, but it can also introduce a degree of digital dependency that has its own stresses and psychological repercussions.

Never have we been so reliant on digital technologies for supplying our everyday needs and our sense of connection to others but increasingly, it is our psychological equilibrium and our ability to be in the present moment that is under assault from digital environments which require us to think in certain ways in order to operate within an 'attention economy'. The recent COVID-19 pandemic has shown just how dependent on internet-enabled forms of digital connection we have become for sustaining our psychological wellbeing.

The idea for this book started life before the pandemic as a short, mixed-methods study looking at how digital dependency could affect the efficacy of mindfulness training. As the pandemic took hold and lockdowns deepened, the face-to-face mindfulness training sessions that were integral to the study got cancelled and everything ground to a halt. At this point, the emphasis of the study shifted to an investigation of the more qualitative aspects of this dynamic, exploring the experiential value of mindfulness in digital contexts, something that had become increasingly relevant as all of life went online. Finally, there was an opportunity to connect my experiential appreciation of mindfulness with my psychology research. This became the seed of the book as it is now.

This book aims to bring some of the experiential wisdom of mindfulness and non-dualism to these (sometimes challenging) digital experiences. As such, it attempts to bring together two different domains from within psychology and speak to both of these audiences—Mindfulness

Practitioners and Psychologists working within the field of Cyberpsychology. In order to bridge this gap, I have used a qualitative approach which acknowledges the value of subjective experience in furthering psychological understanding.

The book should be read as an extended study spread across the entire book with the first two chapters acting as introductions and literature reviews. Chapter 1 introduces the Cyberpsychology angle and proposes a view of digital wellbeing that sees the displacement of attention as being at the heart of digital dependency. Chapter 2 introduces mindfulness and proposes its use as a lens for exploring issues of attention in relation to digital interaction. Chapter 3 reports on sixteen qualitative interviews conducted with those practising mindfulness whilst also being digitally active. This chapter is a combination of methodology and results/analysis sections. The final chapter provides a detailed discussion of the experiences recounted in Chapter 3, exploring a broader contextual understanding of the mindless states that emerge in digital environments and their effects on attention and wellbeing. The chapter concludes with implications for Cyberpsychology research and suggestions for a digital approach to mindfulness practice.

It has been a rare treat for me to connect non-duality to some of my academic research and it provided me with an important sense of purpose during the dark days of the pandemic. I hope that this book manages to combine elements of mindfulness and Cyberpsychology in ways that you find meaningful and that it offers you food for thought whatever your inclination within psychology. On a personal level, I hope it also inspires you to stop for a moment and think about how your attention is being used (and abused) whilst you are engaged in digital interactions.

Brighton, UK   Dave Harley

Acknowledgements

I would like to thank all my interviewees, the Psychology undergraduates, the mindfulness students and their tutors who were all so willing to share their experiences with me and to engage in this project with enthusiasm despite the complications of the COVID-19 pandemic and its lockdowns. I would also like to thank the many students who have taken my Cyberpsychology module over the years, helping me to keep my finger on the pulse of digital innovation as well as helping me to appreciate the social and psychological dilemmas that run alongside these developments. Finally, my biggest thanks go to Robin for her tireless sense-checking and proof reading of my ideas and writing—and for just 'getting it'.

Contents

1 Digital Wellbeing: Making Sense of Digital Dependency   1
   Introduction   2
   How Do Digital Devices Affect Our Psychological Wellbeing?   3
   Should Digital Dependency Be Understood as an Addiction?   7
   Displacement and the Reshaping of Attention   9
   Attending to Attention   10
   Conclusions   16
   References   16

2 Mindfulness in a Digital World   25
   Introduction   26
   What is Mindfulness?   26
   Secular Mindfulness Training   28
   Applying Mindfulness to the Digital Domain   31

The Effect of Mindfulness on Unconscious Digital Habits	34
Conclusions	36
References	36

3 A Qualitative Study of Mindfulness and Digital Practice   43

Introduction	44
Methods	45
Participants	46
Procedure and Context	47
Approach	47
Analysis	48
Findings	49
Integrating Digital and Mindfulness Practices into Everyday Life	49
Conclusions	73
References	73

4 A Digital Approach to Mindfulness   77

Introduction	78
The Effects of Digital Interaction on Attention and Wellbeing	78
Applying Mindfulness to Digital Interaction (Explaining the Dilemma)	79
Dealing with the Digital Imperative	80
Dealing with the Hyper-Real (and Algorithmic) Imperatives	82
Implications for Cyberpsychology	86
The Displacement of Attention Versus the Displacement of Behaviour	86
The Need for the Regulation of Online Behaviour and Algorithms	87
Implications for Mindfulness Training	88
1) An Understanding of Mindfulness Principles	89
2) Digital Self-Awareness—Waking Up to the *Digital Autopilot*	89
3) Techniques for Encouraging Digital Mindfulness	90

Beyond Secular Mindfulness	90
Limitations of This Study	92
The COVID-19 Context	93
References	94
Index	**99**

About the Author

Dr. Dave Harley is a principal lecturer in Psychology at the University of Brighton where he has been teaching modules in Cyberpsychology for over a decade. He is a committee member of the BPS Cyberpsychology Section and his broad research areas cover Cyberpsychology and Human Computer Interaction. He has a historic interest in older people's appropriation of digital technologies, investigating their use of video games, social media, online communities and mobile phones. His current research explores issues relating to the extended digital self. He is a co-author of the 2018 book also published by Palgrave: *Cyberpsychology as Everyday Digital Experience Across the Lifespan*.

1

Digital Wellbeing: Making Sense of Digital Dependency

Abstract This introductory chapter reviews Cyberpsychology research considering the effect of digital technologies on psychological wellbeing. Whilst there are clear benefits that come from being digitally connected, our reliance on them brings its own problems. This chapter explores the downsides of habitual involvement in terms of stress, depression, anxiety and dependency. Current explanations for these negative effects focus on the displacement of healthy behaviour as being the root cause but here an alternative approach is proposed that focuses on the displacement of attention. The attentional challenge of digital technologies is explored by looking at our innate attentional capacities and the demands placed upon them by the expectations of computational interfaces, multitasking and deliberate exploitation by digital designers.

Keywords Mindfulness · Digital interaction · Technostress · Displacement effect · Digital dependency · Digital wellbeing · Digital addiction · Attention · Displacement of attention · Multitasking · Attention economy · Mindlessness · Digital media · Social media

Introduction

Life in the twenty-first century is increasingly governed and mediated by digital networks and devices which filter our experience and supplant ways of being that were once perhaps more immediate and visceral. Just think about how the experience of shopping, dating, reading, playing, studying or listening to music has changed over the last twenty years. These changes have real consequences for how we understand ourselves as human beings, how we relate to the world around us and how we maintain our psychological wellbeing. Everyone who uses digital devices to connect to the internet will be familiar with the strange mixture of wonder and stressful irritation that comes with regular use. The ease with which one can instantly connect to other places in the world, access (obscure) knowledge, people, products and entertainment as well as allowing perpetual connections with those we care about. Digital inclusion appears to bring obvious benefits and why would anyone deny themselves access to such a resource? At the same time, there are the inevitable stresses that come with being digitally connected—one has to deal with complex interfaces that are constantly being updated and revised, one has to deal with the hardware, software and network malfunctions and one has to manage the onslaught of extraneous information and communications that come through the device from people and businesses eager to attract our attention. In psychological research, such stresses are broadly referred to as 'technostress' and are well-known for causing problems including mental fatigue, irritability, disturbed sleep and depression (La Torre et al., 2019). This chapter will look more deeply into the origins of this stress and consider why our psychological wellbeing has become so dependent on digital technology.

Over time, our reliance on the digital world has increased and ongoing access to digital networks is now essential for modern living. In the UK, we spend longer interacting with our digital devices than we do asleep and those of us with mobile phones check them on average every 12 min (OfCom, 2018). As internet penetration reaches saturation point, similar tales of digital dependency are becoming common across Europe (Škařupová et al., 2016), North America (Cheever et al., 2014) and Asia (Mak et al., 2014). The recent Coronavirus pandemic has only served to deepen this dependency with the internet becoming the major source of daily provisions, entertainment and social contact during the various lockdowns (Beaunoyer et al., 2020).

The question for many of us in the developed world now is whether we should accept this emerging digital dependency as a natural evolution of our relationship with these technologies or something that is possibly more damaging. Digital technologies have inserted themselves into the very fabric of our everyday life, presenting us with a myriad of new social and psychological opportunities that rarely fail to engage us but equally challenge our ability to cope with the social and psychological changes that they bring (upsetting the status quo in many areas of our life). Whilst the benefits of being 'perpetually connected' are obvious to most, there is growing concern that our habitual involvement with these devices may be detrimental to our psychological and emotional wellbeing.

In this book, I will consider how the pervasive changes in attention, thought and behaviour that accompany this new digital dependency might be better understood and addressed through a lens of mindfulness.

How Do Digital Devices Affect Our Psychological Wellbeing?

Perhaps the simplest way to consider our relationship with digital technologies is to examine how the amount of time we spend interacting with digital screens is affecting our psychological wellbeing. In a hedonistic way, psychological wellbeing is often used to describe the presence of positive feelings (e.g. happiness or self-esteem) and the absence of negative ones (e.g. depression or anxiety). It is also used in a broader sense to accommodate longstanding feelings of life fulfilment or satisfaction (Deci & Ryan, 2008). In digital environments, these feelings may be prompted by various forms of interaction with content, other people and the technology itself.

'Screen time' studies show that moderate amounts may be beneficial for psychological wellbeing (Przybylski & Weinstein, 2017). However, increasing digital engagement brings a more sedentary lifestyle (Hoare et al., 2016) which is likely to make us more obese, depressed and experience a poorer quality of life (Stiglic & Viner, 2019). As we will see, explanations for why screen time undermines wellbeing in this way centre around the notion of *displacement* (Neuman, 1988), i.e. that digital engagement *displaces* other healthier physical activities that are necessary for maintaining health and wellbeing.

Some of the earliest studies of internet use showed displacement effects occurring as part of the initial adoption of the internet with its use displacing face-to-face social activities and increasing loneliness and depression (Kraut et al., 1998). The importance of social contact is long established as a source of belonging and an essential resource for maintaining psychological wellbeing (Baumeister & Leary, 1995). The internet was shown to be an asocial technology, negating opportunities for in-person social contact that were deemed essential for psychological wellbeing.

Subsequent research with the same sample three years later (Kraut et al., 2002) showed that once families had integrated the internet into their daily lives, displacement effects diminished overall and started to differentiate along the lines of individual sociability. Extraverts would use the internet as a means of amplifying their social opportunities and thereby increase their local community involvement, reversing earlier feelings of loneliness and increasing their self-esteem and positive mood (Kraut et al., 2002). Introverts on the other hand were likely to develop a preference for being online long term because this allowed them to avoid the anxieties they often experienced in face-to-face situations. This still left them feeling lonely and depressed.

The social and interactive possibilities of digital technology have grown enormously since that time, but research continues to show similar wellbeing effects in relation to individual sociability. The so-called 'rich get richer' effect (Kraut et al., 2002) shows sociable extraverts boosting their social involvement on and offline through smartphones (Kim, 2017), social media (Ong et al., 2011) and video games (Reer & Krämer, 2017). Extraverts' gregariousness is also evident in the way that they behave online. On social media, they are more likely to actively participate, engage in public discussions, create their own content and engage with content shared by their friends (e.g. by "liking" them or responding to them) (Bachrach et al., 2012; Bowden-Green et al., 2020). These behaviours seem to result in a 'beneficial' form of digital dependency that brings closeness with friends, online sources of social support, a sense of belonging and increases in life satisfaction (Lin et al., 2018).

In contrast, shy or introverted individuals treat the experience of being online as a form of 'social compensation' (Peter et al., 2005) discovering opportunities for online involvement that further displace their face-to-face social interactions. Introverts are more likely to use the internet for solitary activities or entertainment purposes (Mitchell et al., 2011). Unfortunately, this kind of digital dependency does not seem to lead to emotional closeness or fulfilling relationships and instead leads to lower self-esteem, greater loneliness and depression (Cheng et al., 2019).

This research goes some way to explaining how individual differences in terms of sociability can create divergent forms of digital dependency with sociable extraverts faring better. However, we should be wary of the reductionism in such explanations which suggests that the effects of digital dependency are solely down to the kind of person that you are. It is not so easy to see how digital dependency plays out in a person's life as a simple reflection of one's personality or any fixed sense of sociability. Social life by its very nature is fluid and depends upon the people that we meet and interact with and, when it comes to digital social contact, the way in which the technology honours our social intentions and aspirations.

Trait approaches to personality assume that one's identity endures across different situations determining one's behaviour in a reasonably consistent manner. Unfortunately, the surveys[1] used to assess individual sociability and its effects (e.g. in relation to loneliness) are firmly rooted in face-to-face situations as the litmus test for beneficial social contact and tend to ignore the transformative potential of digital connections. Studies of online behaviour show that we do not always behave in

---

[1] Hidden within this research is an implicit bias towards face-to-face interaction as an indicator of 'healthy' human behaviour—most of the proxy measures used to assess sociability (i.e. extraversion-introversion, loneliness and shyness) use survey questions that prime participants in this way. Example survey questions: *I enjoy social gatherings just to be with people* (Kraut et al., 2002); *My interests and ideas are not shared by those around me* (Kim, 2017); *I shy away from crowds of people* (Ong et al., 2011).

line with the constraints of our offline ('actual') self and may start to explore other aspects of our self online. Particularly in spaces where we are unknown to others and can remain anonymous and unidentifiable, we are likely to become less inhibited and this can lead to us being more altruistic and helpful to strangers or conversely more impulsive, aggressive and abusive to others (Lapidot-Lefler & Barak, 2012). Disinhibition may also bring an attitude of 'identity play' (Valkenburg et al., 2005) or identity reconstruction (Huang et al., 2018) in some online spaces whereby participants feel able to 'try out' personal attributes or traits that they do not possess in the real world. This is particularly true for adolescents seeking to explore different ways of being in relation to others appearing older, different gender, more flirtatious, macho, etc. (Valkenburg et al., 2005).

Despite the displacement of social interaction to online spaces, some shy and introverted individuals actually find a more authentic version of themselves there. The anonymous and controllable interactions that take place within discussion forums and social media offer introverts and shy individuals the space to express themselves freely without fear of being judged and this appears to be irresistible to them (Amichai-Hamburger et al., 2002; Marriott & Buchanan, 2014).

Nonetheless, tying one's wellbeing to digital forms of sociability is inherently risky whatever one's individual orientation to sociability. When one's sense of self and agency in the world relies so heavily on a constant digital connection, any disruption to this (due to a lack of network access, power or low bandwidth) can cause distress and anxiety and temporarily undermine one's psychological wellbeing. This is true for extraverts and introverts alike. Digital interactions have become so embedded in our everyday lives that this phobic reaction is now commonplace and widespread. The advent of the smartphone has accentuated this aspect of digital dependency with the associated stresses and anxieties infiltrating every aspect of our lives. This has led to the phobia being described in terms of nomophobia or *no mo*bile phone *phobia* (King et al., 2013).

An early UK survey of nomophobia showed that 66% of mobile phone users feared losing their mobile phones (SecurEnvoy, 2012). Subsequent studies of nomophobia have shown that feelings of anxiety and worry are common amongst mobile users when they cannot connect to the internet via their smartphone for information or social contact. This is true in all countries where smartphones are widespread and seems to be a particular issue for younger adults. Studies show 42.6% of Turkish university students experience nomophobia (Yildirim et al., 2016); 99.5% of American pharmacy students (with 18.2% experiencing severe symptoms) (Cain Malcom, 2019) and 100% of Indian medical students (Farooqi et al., 2018) (with 22.1% severe).

Attempts to explain nomophobia suggest that the underlying dependency is social in origin primarily driven by a fear of missing out (FoMO) on social opportunities with others online (Kneidinger-Müller, 2019). However, the device itself also plays its part as a source of dependency. Over time and as a result of habitual use, smartphone users start to develop an attachment to the phone as a social entity in its own right (R. Muench & C. Muench, 2020). Regular users start to prioritise attention to their phone over those that are physically nearby whilst engaging in face-to-face conversations (Marty-Dugas et al., 2018) undermining the enjoyment gained from such encounters (Dwyer et al., 2018). They may also start to relate to the phone itself as a digital companion when bored, lonely or socially anxious (Carolus et al., 2019).

Should Digital Dependency Be Understood as an Addiction?

The widespread emergence of nomophobia might suggest some kind of withdrawal effects in relation to a digital 'addiction'. Certainly, digital dependency is increasingly being described as an addiction in much the same way as alcohol or hard-core drugs, incorporating notions such as tolerance and withdrawal to explain increasing shifts to digital dependency in everyday life (e.g. Griffiths, 1999). We see similar tropes in the news (Donnelly, 2019) and in popular discourse: a recent survey in the UK showed that 59% of internet users considered themselves to be 'hooked' on their connected devices (Ofcom, 2016).

The study of internet addiction has a long history within psychology where its acceptance as a clinical diagnosis has long been pursued (e.g.

Griffiths, 2000; Young, 1998) closely followed by addiction to video games (Pontes et al., 2014), social media (Van den Eijnden et al., 2016) and the smartphone (Lin et al., 2016). At a biological level, it does seem that certain forms of digital engagement can activate the pleasure centres of the brain in 'addictive' ways, neurologically reinforcing activities in the same way as other behavioural addictions like gambling (Olsen, 2011). Similar elaboration of dopaminergic pathways in the brain occurs when playing video games (Koepp et al., 1998; Sun et al., 2012), viewing online porn (Love et al., 2015) or when posting about oneself or receiving more likes than others on social media (Meshi et al., 2013).

However, we also know that similar forms of dopamine release underpin our motivation to engage with others as part of normal and natural social bonding (Krach et al., 2010). Dopamine release is part of how we respond to happy (Rademacher et al., 2010) or attractive people (Aharon et al., 2001) and it is there when we discover that other people like or approve of us (Izuma, et al., 2008). It also helps to strengthen loving relationships, being present when we think about the person we love (Aron et al., 2005) and when a mother sees her own baby smiling (Strathearn et al., 2008). If addictive processes are at play within digital interactions, it will be difficult to isolate them as they appear to be hijacking innate human social reflexes.

Whilst digital dependency has potential for affecting psychological wellbeing, it does not follow that we should start to think of it in terms of addiction. Human beings are deeply social and the internet's transformative potential lies in our ability to harness its social opportunities—to discount this would be to ignore its potential for supporting human flourishing. Treating one's acute awareness of one's smartphone or the social media notifications that come through it as addictive would be like describing the way that we maintain eye contact or keep track of the topic of conversation whilst talking with friends as signs of a psychiatric disorder. It runs the risk of pathologising normal everyday behaviour and shifting the emphasis of the problem onto individual users rather than acknowledging the impact of digital design on dependency (and the hidden profit motives that might seek to foster such dependency).

Interestingly digital natives themselves do not even consider their digital dependency as something that is problematic (Ahn & Jung, 2016).

Perhaps, unsurprisingly, there has been great difficulty in establishing widespread acceptance of digital addiction as a psychiatric diagnosis and this has led to the employment of various terms such as problematic or compulsive use of internet/smartphone/social media to capture what is seen to be a dysfunctional shift in everyday behaviour. Here, dysfunctional use may also be viewed as a compensatory strategy used to cope with difficult life circumstances rather than as a genuine addictive behaviour (Kardefelt-Winther, 2014; Schimmenti & Caretti, 2010).

However one defines digital dependency, its potential impact on psychological functioning and wellbeing remains clear. Over time habitual use can develop into an increasing reliance on digital connections where some users start to experience nomophobia when they are disconnected and crave ever greater digital involvement. If unchecked, this can start to creep into other aspects of life, disrupting sleep patterns, causing fatigue and irritability, poor immunity, affecting academic or work performance and causing depression (Mihajlov & Vejmelka, 2017).

Explanations for why digital dependency can have such negative effects on wellbeing again focus on *displacement* as being responsible where increasing use of the digital world for escapism displaces ever more essential activities like work, eating and sleeping (Mihajlov & Vejmelka, 2017).

Displacement and the Reshaping of Attention

So far, we have seen how digital involvement can affect psychological wellbeing both positively through social amplification and negatively through the displacement of physical and social activities. Central to Cyberpsychology's understanding of digital dependency is this notion of displacement and it is worth examining the underlying implications of this term a little further.

The origins of displacement as an explanatory principle date back to the 1950s and 60s when it was used to explain children's 'addiction' to TV in a Freudian sense: excessive TV viewing was understood as a defence mechanism, protecting the ego through a retreat into the fantasy world of TV fiction and away from the perceived threats of intra-family conflict and other difficult social relationships (Schramm et al., 1961). However, current uses of the term 'displacement' within Cyberpsychology (e.g. Cheng et al., 2019; Kraut et al., 1998) consider the preferential shift to digital interaction as an act of mere *convenient substitution* where time previously spent on one activity is now redirected to another (digital one). Displacement has become a shallow descriptive term that accounts for the overt and gross behavioural decisions that determine the amount of time spent on digital versus 'real-life' activities. It no longer seeks to identify underlying human drives that may cause this shift, nor does it unearth any direct 'effects' except through negative causation, i.e. the assertion that the absence of real-life activities is always detrimental.

What lies at the heart of displacement remains largely unexamined and in this book, I will seek to re-examine displacement not as an issue of activity but as an issue of attention, i.e. as an emergent recalibration process taking place not just at a behavioural level but also at the subtler level of attention.

Attending to Attention

It is within the attentional field of immediate digital experience that the possibilities for digital wellbeing are encountered, and behavioural habits formed and resisted (for better or worse). At a personal level, the nature of digital engagement is mostly provisional, driven perhaps by prior intentions and deliberate choices but also infinitely challenged, subverted and dissipated by other forces at play in the digital world: the social demands of others online; the informational demands of the web and the 'designed for' distractions from advertising and entertainment media (Fogg, 2003).

Maintaining one's digital wellbeing has become a necessary life skill for those living in developed nations and this involves taking care of one's own attentional capacities, recognising how one allocates attentional resources to the digital world and becoming aware of how digital dependency may be affecting the rest of one's life (Vanden Abeele, 2020). Whilst moderate amounts of digital engagement may be beneficial (Przybylski & Weinstein, 2017), it is clear that the social, entertainment and informational rewards that come through digital connection can quickly establish habits that start to dominate attention and undermine our ability to be present in the 'real' world (Ward et al., 2017). If we want to understand the detrimental effects of digital dependency, it therefore makes sense for us to start by considering attention.

Once we start to inhabit networked digital environments on a regular basis and live our lives through them, our attention is necessarily reshaped to accommodate the mediated representations that operate there. Thanks to the neuroplasticity of our brains, we can adapt quite readily to such environments (depending on our age and cognitive capacity) and learn to treat particular forms of digital representation as if they were proxies for the real world. During this process, we become sensitised to mediated expressions of information and interaction that stretch our attentional capacities in significant ways. The speed and parallel nature of processing within modern computers and digital networks easily surpass the capacity of our own human brains.[2] As a result, digital connections accelerate symbolic interactions and encourage divisions of attention across multiple, continuous and simultaneous domains. Control of our own attention becomes essential if we want to manage the potential sensory and informational overload that comes through the digital world without it overwhelming us. We develop our own techniques for managing the attentional demands of digital environments whilst (hopefully) continuing to reap the rewards. Understanding how we manage this is therefore essential if we are to understand how these environments impact psychological wellbeing.

Before considering the Cyberpsychology research on attention, it is worth noting that attention itself remains a difficult concept for psychologists to define and agree upon (Styles, 2005). There appear to be quite distinct modes of attention that operate depending upon specific circumstances and our relationship to those circumstances. At

---

[2] The average speed of data transfer in the UK internet is currently 64 Megabytes per second (Ofcom, 2018) compared with just 0.00125 Mbps for visual data to the human brain (Anderson et al., 2005).

one extreme, we have an open awareness of our embodied experience in every situation that monitors the immediate environment and our physiological response to it (bottom-up, stimulus-driven attention). This remains mostly unconscious until something novel, dangerous or personally relevant appears at which point it is 'brought' to our attention. At the other extreme of our attentional abilities is the domain of focused attention which drives our conscious choices and provides an analytic assessment of our current situation (top-down, goal-directed attention) (McGilchrist, 2019).

Research within the field of Cyberpsychology has so far pursued a mostly cognitive (top-down) perspective on attention, using an information processing model to identify the processing limitations of focal attention in terms of attentional bottlenecks and considering how digital users manage these through *executive* or *cognitive control*, employing attention, working memory and goal management to deal with digital environments successfully (Gazzaley & Rosen, 2016).

Multitasking (or engaging in two or more tasks at once) is a very common way that we attempt to manage the competing demands of digital environments (Loh & Kanai, 2016). However, despite its apparent acceptance and appeal as a tactic for greater productivity in our work and home lives, we find it very difficult to split our attention in this way, especially when tasks are cognitively taxing (Gazzaley & Rosen, 2016). In the real world, we can rely on a degree of unconscious embodied awareness to keep track of our immediate environment whilst simultaneously engaging in cognitive tasks (so, for instance, you can walk down the street and avoid the traffic whilst acknowledging a neighbour with a wave and at the same time be giving directions to a friend by speaking on your mobile phone).

However, this is not possible in digital environments where embodied acts of unconscious awareness must be translated into overt cognitive tasks that require focal attention and this creates direct competition for attentional resources 'at the interface' (think about a comparable online scenario where you are navigating your avatar down a virtual street in Grand Theft Auto whilst responding to a friend who has appeared on Messenger and at the same time texting directions to another friend on your phone using Whatsapp—a more tricky scenario).

What we actually do in digital environments is best described as 'rapid task switching', shifting our attention between different online activities, websites, apps, devices as well as the demands of the real world in order to keep track of our progress on different tasks and to maintain our involvement in ongoing communications and relationships (Kirschner & De Bruyckere, 2017). The digital world is a place of constant interruption and distraction where even the act of just being oneself becomes a cognitive task rather than a living embodied experience.

Whilst interruptions may be preferred by some (e.g. as a relief from boredom), they more often than not come at a cost to our productivity and socio-emotional functioning (van der Schuur et al., 2015), slowing us down, increasing the errors we make (Payne et al., 2007) and making us socially anxious and depressed (Becker et al., 2013). Every interruption we experience disrupts our train of thought or workflow making it harder for us to recover our initial focus. Information workers who spend their working lives immersed in digital environments switch tasks on average every 5 minutes and only return to the original task 70% of the time (Dabbish et al., 2011). Students completing academic work switch tasks at a similar rate (every 5.6 minutes) with competition coming from social media and texting (Rosen et al., 2013). Media multitasking has become ubiquitous and over time this repeated disruption can undermine the ability to sustain focused attention on single activities (Ralph et al., 2015) and to direct attention deliberately (Ophir et al., 2009). This suggests that something more crucial than the displacement of activity is taking place here and it has to do with how digital environments challenge control of our own attention. Digital wellbeing becomes about how we stay in control.

One of the ways that we compensate for the impact of interruptions is to increase the speed with which we complete our digital tasks, keeping our text messages short and to the point, skim reading online content, etc. (Entschew, 2021). Unfortunately, this just increases levels of stress, frustration and anxiety (Mark et al., 2008).

Another way that we deal with the informational overload of the digital world is through *selective attention*: separating out only the most important and relevant of on-screen stimuli to pay attention to (e.g. distinguishing important personal emails from the mass of spam). This capacity relies on memory to sensitise us to the appearance of certain stimuli over others. In the digital context, this allows us to prioritise tasks and maintain conscious control over our own attention and digital activities (i.e. it is a top-down process). This ability pays dividends in terms of making us more productive and reducing interruption-induced stress (Tams et al., 2015) and some forms of digital interaction (e.g. action video games) even seem to improve this ability (Hubert-Wallander et al., 2011). However, studies show that deliberate forms of selective attention start to wane in the midst of heavy media multitasking and a more unconscious and reactive attentional stance starts to emerge driven by innate bottom-up responses (Ralph et al., 2014). Given the increasing prevalence of heavy media multitasking, this perhaps indicates a growing 'mindless' trend in relation to digital interaction.

Thanks to the advent of mobile computing and smartphones, we see this same unconscious attentional vigilance spreading beyond the digital world and into 'real' life where an ongoing and automatic awareness has developed in relation to online activity. This is evident through permanent cognitive involvement with online concerns in the midst of real life (Reinecke et al., 2018), constant checking behaviours (Bayer et al., 2016) and the experience of phantom smartphone vibrations (Rosenberger, 2015). The mere presence of a smartphone colonises our unconscious attention undermining our cognitive reserves (Ward et al., 2017).

There are aspects of the internet and the way that it has developed over the last 30 years that further emphasise and exploit this mindlessness, presenting content and forms of interaction that connect with these innate and unconscious tendencies, steering us down metaphorical rabbit holes. Thanks to our evolutionary heritage, we human beings are unconsciously primed to pay attention to the following (although this is not an exhaustive list):

a) Novelty—as human beings we always pay attention to things that we have not encountered before in our environment, and this has had important survival value in our past. This is an attentional bias that we are born with (Slater et al., 1984) and as we all know the internet has an almost infinite capacity for presenting novel information and content to us.

b) Threat—a large part of our innate and unconscious awareness in our immediate environment is concerned with identifying and responding to threats. Indeed, the whole of the autonomic nervous system has evolved for this purpose (Matthews et al., 1997). Fear and the stress response play a part in many aspects of digital experience from our auditory sensitivity to notification sounds, our reactions to colour (e.g. red) in interfaces and our inability to ignore violent and provocative online content.

c) Relating to other people—social bonding is essential for human beings to feel a sense of security as this has been integral to our success as a species. As infants, we already have an innate tendency to take notice of human faces (Leppänen, 2016) and to seek belonging and social approval. We have an attentional bias towards happy faces (Wirth & Wentura, 2020) and appear to recognise consciousness in others and reciprocal attention (Nagy, 2008). The pervasive and promiscuous social connections of the internet and social media capitalise on this tendency, encouraging us to post self-generated content, connect with others and chase symbols of social worth such as likes.

d) Ourselves—alertness increases when we are presented with information that obviously relates to us (Sui & Rotshtein, 2019). Digital systems capitalise on this tendency by personalising our interactions with them through the use of digital profiles. Addressing us by name and tailoring content to suit our anticipated interests encourages us to treat them as if they had an imminent awareness of who we are (Cotter et al., 2022).

In the age of the attention economy, digital designers and advertisers have learned to exploit these attentional vulnerabilities still further, designing content and interactions that enlist these innate responses as part of media multitasking. Search and media algorithms learn our preferences from these unconscious attentional biases creating a self-perpetuating cycle. All of this hijacking our innate attentional bias at an unconscious level—it is perhaps no surprise that so many people feel overwhelmed, addicted and out of control. In order to take back control of our own attention, it is necessary to become aware of this pervasive unconscious mode of interaction and reinstate the processes of reflection and deliberation that will allow us to continue benefiting from the digital world.

Conclusions

This chapter has shown how digital technologies have become intimately tied to our psychological wellbeing and whilst the benefits remain clear, the digital revolution has come at a cost to our experiences of everyday stress, anxiety and depression. So far psychological approaches have focused on the displacement of healthy activity as the way to understand this issue. This chapter has invited a different way of approaching this dilemma by focusing on the reshaping of attention that underpins everyday activities in the digital era. Psychological research on attention has so far used the information processing model to reveal the objective constraints of attention in relation to the digital world and establish a shift towards an unconscious mindless form of interaction that occurs as a result of increasing media multitasking. In the next chapter, we explore how mindfulness might offer an alternative lens which will do just that.

References

Adler, R. F., & Benbunan-Fich, R. (2012). Juggling on a high wire: Multitasking effects on performance. *International Journal of Human-Computer Studies, 70*(2), 156–168.

Aharon, I., Etcoff, N., Ariely, D., Chabris, C. F., O'connor, E., & Breiter, H. C. (2001). Beautiful faces have variable reward value: FMRI and behavioral evidence. *Neuron, 32*(3), 537–551.

Ahn, J., & Jung, Y. (2016). The common sense of dependence on smartphone: A comparison between digital natives and digital immigrants. *New Media & Society, 18*(7), 1236–1256.

Amichai-Hamburger, Y., Wainapel, G., & Fox, S. (2002). On the Internet no one knows I'm an introvert: Extroversion, neuroticism, and Internet interaction. *Cyberpsychology & behavior, 5*(2), 125–128.

Anderson, C. H., Van Essen, D. C., & Olshausen, B. A. (2005). Directed visual attention and the dynamic control of information flow. In *Neurobiology of attention* (pp. 11–17). Academic Press.

Aron, A., Fisher, H., Mashek, D. J., Strong, G., Li, H., & Brown, L. L. (2005). Reward, motivation, and emotion systems associated with early-stage intense romantic love. *Journal of Neurophysiology, 94*, 327–337.

Bachrach, Y., Kosinski, M., Graepel, T., Kohli, P., & Stillwell, D. (2012, June). Personality and patterns of Facebook usage. In *Proceedings of the 4th Annual ACM Web Science Conference*, 24–32.

Baumeister, R. F., & Leary, M. R. (1995). The need to belong: Desire for interpersonal attachments as a fundamental human motivation. *Psychological Bulletin, 117*, 497–529.

Bayer, J. B., Dal Cin, S., Campbell, S. W., & Panek, E. (2016). Consciousness and self-regulation in mobile communication. *Human Communication Research, 42*(1), 71–97.

Beaunoyer, E., Dupéré, S., & Guitton, M. J. (2020). COVID-19 and digital inequalities: Reciprocal impacts and mitigation strategies. *Computers in Human Behavior, 111*, 106424.

Becker, M. W., Alzahabi, R., & Hopwood, C. J. (2013). Media multitasking is associated with symptoms of depression and social anxiety. *Cyberpsychology, Behavior, and Social Networking, 16*(2), 132–135.

Berryman, C., Ferguson, C. J., & Negy, C. (2018). Social media use and mental health among young adults. *Psychiatric Quarterly, 89*(2), 307–314.

Bowden-Green, T., Hinds, J., & Joinson, A. (2020). How is extraversion related to social media use? A literature review. *Personality and Individual Differences, 164*, 110040.

Cain, J., & Malcom, D. R. (2019). An assessment of pharmacy students' psychological attachment to smartphones at two colleges of pharmacy. *American Journal of Pharmaceutical Education, 83*(7).

Carolus, A., Binder, J. F., Muench, R., Schmidt, C., Schneider, F., & Buglass, S. L. (2019). Smartphones as digital companions: Characterizing the relationship between users and their phones. *New Media & Society, 21*(4), 914–938.

Cheever, N. A., Rosen, L. D., Carrier, L. M., & Chavez, A. (2014). Out of sight is not out of mind: The impact of restricting wireless mobile device use on anxiety levels among low, moderate and high users. *Computers in Human Behavior, 37*, 290–297.

Cheng, C., Wang, H. Y., Sigerson, L., & Chau, C. L. (2019). Do the socially rich get richer? A nuanced perspective on social network site use and online social capital accrual. *Psychological Bulletin, 145*(7), 734.

Cotter, K., DeCook, J. R., Kanthawala, S., & Foyle, K. (2022). In FYP We Trust: The Divine Force of Algorithmic Conspirituality. *International Journal of Communication, 16*, 1–23.

Dabbish, L., Mark, G., & Gonzalez, V. (2011). Why do I keep interrupting myself? Environment, habit and self-interruption. In *Proceedings of the 2011 Annual Conference on Human Factors in, Computing Systems*, 3127–3130.

Deci, E. L., & Ryan, R. M. (2008). Hedonia, eudaimonia, and well-being: An introduction. *Journal of Happiness Studies, 9*(1), 1–11.

Donnelly, L. (2019, January 10). Social media addicts behave like those addicted to drink and drugs. *The Telegraph*. Retrieved from: https://www.telegraph.co.uk/

Dwyer, R. J., Kushlev, K., & Dunn, E. W. (2018). Smartphone use undermines enjoyment of face-to-face social interactions. *Journal of Experimental Social Psychology, 78*, 233–239.

Entschew, E. M. (2021). Acceleration through digital communication: Theorizing on a perceived lack of tisme. *Humanistic Management Journal, 6*(2), 273–287.

Farooqui, I. A., Pore, P., & Gothankar, J. (2018). Nomophobia: An emerging issue in medical institutions? *Journal of Mental Health, 27*(5), 438–441.

Fogg, B. J. (2003). *Persuasive Technology: Using Computers to Change What We Think and Do*. Morgan Kaufmann.

Gazzaley, A., & Rosen, L. D. (2016). *The distracted mind: Ancient brains in a high-tech world*. Mit Press.

Griffiths, M. (1999). Internet addiction: Fact or fiction? *The psychologist*.

Griffiths, M. (2000). Does Internet and computer "addiction" exist? Some case study evidence. *CyberPsychology and Behavior, 3*(2), 211–218.

Hoare, E., Milton, K., Foster, C., & Allender, S. (2016). The associations between sedentary behaviour and mental health among adolescents: A systematic review. *International Journal of Behavioral Nutrition and Physical Activity, 13*(1), 1–22.

Huang, J., Kumar, S., & Hu, C. (2018). Gender differences in motivations for identity reconstruction on social network sites. *International Journal of Human-Computer Interaction, 34*(7), 591–602.

Hubert-Wallander, B., Green, C. S., & Bavelier, D. (2011). Stretching the limits of visual attention: The case of action video games. *Wiley Interdisciplinary Reviews: Cognitive Science, 2*(2), 222–230.

Izuma, K., Saito, D. N., & Sadato, N. (2008). Processing of social and monetary rewards in the human striatum. *Neuron, 58*(2), 284–294.

Kardefelt-Winther, D. (2014). A conceptual and methodological critique of internet addiction research: Towards a model of compensatory internet use. *Computers in Human Behavior, 31*, 351–354.

Kim, J. H. (2017). Smartphone-mediated communication vs. face-to-face interaction: Two routes to social support and problematic use of smartphone. *Computers in Human Behavior, 67*, 282–291.

King, A. L. S., Valença, A. M., Silva, A. C. O., Baczynski, T., Carvalho, M. R., & Nardi, A. E. (2013). Nomophobia: Dependency on virtual environments or social phobia? *Computers in Human Behavior, 29*(1), 140–144.

Kirschner, P. A., & De Bruyckere, P. (2017). The myths of the digital native and the multitasker. *Teaching and Teacher Education, 67*, 135–142.

Kneidinger-Müller, B. (2019). When the smartphone goes offline: A factorial survey of smartphone users' experiences of mobile unavailability. *Computers in Human Behavior, 98*, 1–10.

Koepp, M. J., Gunn, R. N., Lawrence, A. D., Cunningham, V. J., Dagher, A., Jones, T., et al. (1998). Evidence for striatal dopamine release during a video game. *Nature, 393*, 266–268.

Krach, S., Paulus, F. M., Bodden, M., & Kircher, T. (2010). The rewarding nature of social interactions. *Frontiers in Behavioral Neuroscience, 4*, 22.

Kraut, R., Patterson, M., Lundmark, V., Kiesler, S., Mukophadhyay, T., & Scherlis, W. (1998). Internet paradox: A social technology that reduces social involvement and psychological well-being? *American Psychologist, 53*(9), 1017.

Kraut, R., Kiesler, S., Boneva, B., Cummings, J., Helgeson, V., & Crawford, A. (2002). Internet paradox revisited. *Journal of Social Issues, 58*(1), 49–74.

La Torre, G., Esposito, A., Sciarra, I., & Chiappetta, M. (2019). Definition, symptoms and risk of techno-stress: A systematic review. *International Archives of Occupational and Environmental Health, 92*(1), 13–35.

Lapidot-Lefler, N., & Barak, A. (2012). Effects of anonymity, invisibility, and lack of eye-contact on toxic online disinhibition. *Computers in Human Behavior, 28*(2), 434–443.

Leppänen, J. M. (2016). Using eye tracking to understand infants' attentional bias for faces. *Child Development Perspectives, 10*(3), 161–165.

Lin, Y. H., Chiang, C. L., Lin, P. H., Chang, L. R., Ko, C. H., Lee, Y. H., & Lin, S. H. (2016). Proposed diagnostic criteria for smartphone addiction. *PLoS ONE, 11*(11), e0163010.

Lin, X., Su, W., & Potenza, M. N. (2018). Development of an online and offline integration hypothesis for healthy internet use: Theory and preliminary evidence. *Frontiers in Psychology, 9*, 492.

Loh, K. K., & Kanai, R. (2016). How has the Internet reshaped human cognition? *The Neuroscientist, 22*(5), 506–520.

Love, T., Laier, C., Brand, M., Hatch, L., & Hajela, R. (2015). Neuroscience of Internet pornography addiction: A review and update. *Behavioral Sciences, 5*(3), 388–433.

Mak, K. K., Lai, C. M., Watanabe, H., Kim, D. I., Bahar, N., Ramos, M., ... & Cheng, C. (2014). Epidemiology of internet behaviors and addiction among adolescents in six Asian countries. *Cyberpsychology, Behavior, and Social Networking, 17*(11), 720–728.

Mark, G., Gudith, D., & Klocke, U. (2008, April). The cost of interrupted work: more speed and stress. In *Proceedings of the SIGCHI Conference on Human Factors in Computing Systems*, 107–110.

Marriott, T. C., & Buchanan, T. (2014). The True Self Online: Personality Correlates of Preference for Self-Expression Online, and Observer Ratings of Personality Online and Offline. *Computers in Human Behavior, 32*, 171–177.

Marty-Dugas, J., Ralph, B. C., Oakman, J. M., & Smilek, D. (2018). The relation between smartphone use and everyday inattention. *Psychology of Consciousness: Theory, Research, and Practice, 5*(1), 46.

Mathews, A., Mackintosh, B., & Fulcher, E. P. (1997). Cognitive biases in anxiety and attention to threat. *Trends in Cognitive Sciences, 1*(9), 340–345.

McGilchrist, I. (2019). *The master and his emissary*. Yale University Press.

Meshi, D., Morawetz, C., & Heekeren, H. R. (2013). Nucleus accumbens response to gains in reputation for the self relative to gains for others predicts social media use. *Frontiers in Human Neuroscience, 7*, 439.

Mihajlov, M., & Vejmelka, L. (2017). Internet addiction: A review of the first twenty years. *Psychiatria Danubina, 29*(3), 260–272.

Mitchell, M. E., Lebow, J. R., Uribe, R., Grathouse, H., & Shoger, W. (2011). Internet use, happiness, social support and introversion: A more fine grained analysis of person variables and internet activity. *Computers in Human Behavior, 27*(5), 1857–1861.

Muench, R., & Muench, C. (2020, July). Me without my smartphone? Never! Predictors of willingness for smartphone separation and Nomophobia. In *International conference on human-computer interaction* (pp. 217–223). Springer.

Nagy, E. (2008). Innate intersubjectivity: Newborns' sensitivity to communication disturbance. *Developmental Psychology, 44*(6), 1779.

Neuman, S. B. (1988). The displacement effect: Assessing the relation between television viewing and reading performance. *Reading Research Quarterly, 23*, 414–440.

Ofcom (2016). *Communications Market Report 2016*, Ofcom.

Ofcom (2018). *Communications Market Report 2018*, Ofcom.

Olsen, C. M. (2011). Natural rewards, neuroplasticity, and non-drug addictions. *Neuropharmacology, 61*(7), 1109–1122.

Ong, E. Y., Ang, R. P., Ho, J. C., Lim, J. C., Goh, D. H., Lee, C. S., & Chua, A. Y. (2011). Narcissism, extraversion and adolescents' self-presentation on Facebook. *Personality and Individual Differences, 50*(2), 180–185.

Ophir, E., Nass, C., & Wagner, A. D. (2009). Cognitive control in media multitaskers. *Proceedings of the National Academy of Sciences, 106*(37), 15583–15587.

Parry, D. A., & le Roux, D. B. (2019). Media multitasking and cognitive control: A systematic review of interventions. *Computers in Human Behavior, 92*, 316–327.

Payne, S. J., Duggan, G. B., & Neth, H. (2007). Discretionary task interleaving: Heuristics for time allocation in cognitive foraging. *Journal of Experimental Psychology: General, 136*(3), 370.

Peter, J., Valkenburg, P. M., & Schouten, A. P. (2005). Developing a model of adolescent friendship formation on the Internet. *CyberPsychology & Behavior, 8*(5), 423–430.

Pontes, H. M., Kiraly, O., Demetrovics, Z., & Griffiths, M. D. (2014). The conceptualisation and measurement of DSM-5 Internet Gaming Disorder: The development of the IGD-20 Test. *PLoS ONE, 9*(10), e110137.

Przybylski, A. K., & Weinstein, N. (2017). A large-scale test of the goldilocks hypothesis: Quantifying the relations between digital-screen use and the mental well-being of adolescents. *Psychological Science, 28*(2), 204–215.

Rademacher, L., Krach, S., Kohls, G., Irmak, A., Gründer, G., & Spreckelmeyer, K. N. (2010). Dissociation of neural networks for anticipation and consumption of monetary and social rewards. *NeuroImage, 49*(4), 3276–3285.

Ralph, B. C., Thomson, D. R., Cheyne, J. A., & Smilek, D. (2014). Media multitasking and failures of attention in everyday life. *Psychological Research Psychologische Forschung, 78*(5), 661–669.

Ralph, B. C., Thomson, D. R., Seli, P., Carriere, J. S., & Smilek, D. (2015). Media multitasking and behavioral measures of sustained attention. *Attention, Perception, & Psychophysics, 77*(2), 390–401.

Reer, F., & Krämer, N. C. (2017). The connection between introversion/extraversion and social capital outcomes of playing World of Warcraft. *Cyberpsychology, Behavior, and Social Networking, 20*(2), 97–103.

Reich, S. (2010). Adolescents' sense of community on MySpace and Facebook: A mixed methods approach. *Journal of Community Psychology, 38*(6), 688–705.

Reinecke, L., Klimmt, C., Meier, A., Reich, S., Hefner, D., Knop-Huelss, K., & Vorderer, P. (2018). Permanently online and permanently connected: Development and validation of the Online Vigilance Scale. *PLoS ONE, 13*(10), e0205384.

Rosen, L. D., Carrier, L. M., & Cheever, N. A. (2013). Facebook and texting made me do it: Media-induced task-switching while studying. *Computers in Human Behavior, 29*(3), 948–958.

Rosenberger, R. (2015). An experiential account of phantom vibration syndrome. *Computers in Human Behavior, 52*, 124–131.

Schramm, W., Lyle, J., & Parker, E. B. (1961). *Television in the lives of our children.* Stanford University Press.

Schimmenti, A., & Caretti, V. (2010). Psychic retreats or psychic pits?: Unbearable states of mind and technological addiction. *Psychoanalytic Psychology, 27*(2), 115.

SecurEnvoy. (2012). *66% of the population suffer from Nomophobia the fear of being without their phone.* https://www.securenvoy.com/en-gb/blog/66-population-suffer-nomophobia-fear-being-without-their-phone, Accessed 21 November 2020.

Škařupová, K., Ólafsson, K., & Blinka, L. (2016). The effect of smartphone use on trends in European adolescents' excessive Internet use. *Behaviour & Information Technology, 35*(1), 68–74.

Slater, A., Morison, V., & Rose, D. (1984). Habituation in the newborn. *Infant Behavior and Development, 7*(2), 183–200.

Stiglic, N., & Viner, R. M. (2019). Effects of screentime on the health and well-being of children and adolescents: a systematic review of reviews. *BMJ open, 9*(1), e023191.

Strathearn, L., Li, J., Fonagy, P., & Montague, P. R. (2008). What's in a smile? Maternal brain responses to infant facial cues. *Pediatrics, 122*(1), 40–51.

Styles, E. A. (2005). *Attention, perception and memory: An integrated introduction.* Psychology Press.

Sui, J., & Rotshtein, P. (2019). Self-prioritization and the attentional systems. *Current Opinion in Psychology, 29*, 148–152.

Sun, Y., Ying, H., Seetohul, R. M., Xuemei, W., Ya, Z., Qian, L., Guoqing, X., & Ye, S. (2012). Brain fMRIstudy of crave induced by cue pictures in online game addicts (maleadolescents). *Behavioural Brain Research, 233*(2), 563–576.

Tams, S., Thatcher, J., Grover, V., & Pak, R. (2015). Selective attention as a protagonist in contemporary workplace stress: Implications for the interruption age. *Anxiety, Stress, & Coping, 28*(6), 663–686.

Valkenburg, P. M., Schouten, A. P., & Peter, J. (2005). Adolescents' identity experiments on the Internet. *New Media & Society, 7*(3), 383–402.

Vanden Abeele, M. M. P. (2020). Digital wellbeing as a dynamic construct. *Communication Theory*, qtaa024.

Van den Eijnden, R. J., Lemmens, J. S., & Valkenburg, P. M. (2016). The social media disorder scale. *Computers in Human Behavior, 61*, 478–487.

Van Der Schuur, W. A., Baumgartner, S. E., Sumter, S. R., & Valkenburg, P. M. (2015). The consequences of media multitasking for youth: A review. *Computers in Human Behavior, 53*, 204–215.

Ward, A. F., Duke, K., Gneezy, A., & Bos, M. W. (2017). Brain drain: The mere presence of one's own smartphone reduces available cognitive capacity. *Journal of the Association for Consumer Research, 2*(2), 140–154.

Wirth, B. E., & Wentura, D. (2020). It occurs after all: Attentional bias towards happy faces in the dot-probe task. *Attention, Perception, & Psychophysics, 82*, 2463–2481.

World Health Organization. (2019). *World health statistics 2019: Monitoring health for the SDGs, sustainable development goals*. World Health Organization. https://apps.who.int/iris/handle/10665/324835.

Yildirim, C., Sumuer, E., Adnan, M., & Yildirim, S. (2016). A growing fear: Prevalence of nomophobia among Turkish college students. *Information Development, 32*(5), 1322–1331.

Young, K. S. (1998). Internet addiction: The emergence of a new clinical disorder. *Cyberpsychology & Behavior, 1*(3), 237–244.

2

Mindfulness in a Digital World

Abstract This chapter introduces mindfulness as a philosophy and practice, tracing its origins back to ancient Hindu and Buddhist scriptures and its recent development as an applied form of psychological therapy. The practices that typify contemporary mindfulness programmes are outlined along with their potential for exploring issues of attention in relation to digital interactions. Of particular interest here is the ability of mindfulness practice to encourage awareness of unconscious digital habits that often accompany the negative effects of digital dependency. Finally, mindfulness is proposed as a lens for investigating the process by which attentional issues are resolved in digital contexts.

Keywords Mindfulness · Buddhism · Sati · MBSR · MBCT · Mindfulness practice · Decentring · Rumination · Attentional control · Unconscious digital habits

Introduction

It seems that regaining control over one's own attention has become an essential skill if we want to inhabit the digital world whilst at the same time flourish in the rest of our lives. In this chapter, we explore how mindfulness might be useful in getting to grips with this shift in attentional habits and offer a foundational perspective from which to view our emerging digital dependencies. The origins of mindfulness as a philosophy and practice can be traced back to ancient Hindu and Buddhist scripture and here, we consider what this is and how it has developed into an applied form of psychological therapy. The practices that typify contemporary mindfulness programmes are outlined and the relationship of mindfulness to the digital world is explored.

What is Mindfulness?

The term mindfulness was first used in its current form at the end of the nineteenth century as a translation for the Pali word *sati* (Rhys Davids, 1881). The Buddha's earliest teachings presented sati as a way of paying attention and of remembering, or keeping in mind, the focus of contemplation or meditation (Gethin, 2015). In Buddhist doctrine, this faculty is viewed as fundamental to understanding the delusion that pervades human existence: that one is a separate and independent entity: an individual self. Sati is a quality of inner awareness that is essential for Buddhists to inquire into the 'true' nature of being in the world with a view to 'awakening' from one's normal deluded state and end the suffering (or dukkha) that this creates for oneself and all other beings.

Sati exists within the context of Buddhist thought and as such is one of five spiritual faculties regarded as fundamental to the Buddhist path to enlightenment: the others being faith, vigour, concentration and wisdom. The development of sati (or mindfulness) takes place in conjunction with seven other practices that together form the 'noble eightfold path': involving right view, right resolve, right speech, right conduct, right livelihood, right effort, right sati (mindfulness) and right samadhi (absorption in meditation) (Gethin, 2015). Together these practices are concerned with establishing an experiential and ethical framework through which to encounter the world and to nurture compassionate relationships with all other beings.

Within the Buddhist tradition, mindfulness is an invitation for initiates to develop their attentional capacities beyond self-centred activity and thought. 'Pure' undivided attention on a meditative object is seen to provide opportunities for experiencing without the need for an intervening self. Meditative objects are numerous and can be the breath, the body, death or the cultivation of loving kindness to others (Bodhi, 2011).

Mindfulness as a contemporary therapeutic practice has been stripped of its Buddhist connotations and emphasises only 'bare attention' as a means of addressing individual suffering (Thera, 1962). As such it involves engaging with immediate and mundane experience as the focus for attention and doing so whilst resting at the level of sense perception rather than resorting to any kind of intellectual analysis or cognitive labelling. Its use as a form of psychological therapy originates in the work of Jon Kabat-Zinn who started using mindfulness meditation as an approach to pain management whilst working with chronic pain sufferers at the University of Massachusetts Medical Centre (Kabat-Zinn, 1982). Kabat-Zinn's approach employed observation of the breath, simple body awareness and yoga postures to develop participants' mindfulness over the course of 10 weeks, encouraging his participants to become aware of their own pain in a more detached manner without trying to make sense of it or avoid it. This approach which later became known as "mindfulness-based stress reduction" (MBSR) consistently showed significant pain relief and reductions in accompanying mood disturbances (Kabat-Zinn, 1982, 1985; Randolph et al., 1999). Once established as an approach, it also offered a blueprint for those wishing to address other psychological conditions without pharmaceutical intervention or extensive talking therapy. It paved the way for mindfulness-based therapeutic approaches such as Mindfulness Based Cognitive Therapy (MBCT) (Segal et al., 2002), Acceptance and Commitment Therapy (Hayes et al., 2011) and Dialectical Behaviour Therapy (Dimeff & Linehan, 2001). Countless programmes have now been set up adopting Kabat-Zinn's basic principles of mindfulness to deal with stress, anxiety and depression

(Hoffman et al., 2010), as well as other conditions such as substance use and addiction (Brewer et al., 2009).

Mindfulness within this contemporary frame encourages an open awareness of the here and now by "paying attention in a particular way: on purpose, in the present moment, and nonjudgmentally" (Kabat-Zinn, 1994, p.4). Buddhist aspirations of realising the true nature of the self are dropped. Other proponents of mindfulness present it more plainly as "a form of self-regulation of attention" (Bishop et al., 2004, p. 232) or even just "attentional control" (MBCT; Teasdale et al., 1995).

Secular Mindfulness Training

Typically, mindfulness as a therapeutic practice is taught in small groups of up to 30 people over the course of 8 to 10 weeks with each group meeting with a trained mindfulness tutor for a couple of hours a week to learn these new ways of paying attention to their immediate experience. Simple activities (or 'meditations') which focus on bodily sensation are initially used to develop participants' ability in directing and sustaining their own attention in the here and now. Activities include breathing, walking and the 'body scan' (where participants direct their attention to sensations in different parts of their body in a sequence) as well as fully experiencing small objects (by, for example, holding and then eating a raisin). Participants are encouraged to engage with these activities as if they were experiencing them for the first time and to merely observe the sensations that occur without judgement or intellectualisation. The emphasis here is on maintaining single-pointed attention on immediate physical sensations, bringing the mind back to the chosen focus when it wanders and allowing distracting thoughts to come and go without feeling the need to act upon them in any way. Of course, learning to pay attention in this way is challenging and it can take some practise to get to grips with. Once this basic approach to mindfulness has been learnt, participants are asked to extend its use beyond the group meetings and into the rest of their lives using everyday opportunities such as cooking, washing, brushing their teeth, etc. The intention here is to embed mindfulness as an intrinsic element of their everyday life rather than as a separate activity. At the same time, participants are encouraged to continue practising the more formal meditation practices at home (for 45 minutes a day, 6 days a week). As they work through the course, participants are encouraged to share the experience of these activities with other group members through discussion within meetings.

As the course progresses, participants are taught to enlist mindfulness when confronted with more difficult or challenging situations in their daily lives with a view to 'inhabiting the present moment' as a universal coping strategy. The nature of the challenge is likely to vary depending upon the person and whilst it may relate to the situations of pain, illness, stress, anxiety, depression, etc. that initially brought them to the course, it may also involve other difficult feelings. It is this targeted application of mindfulness that shifts the emphasis beyond traditional Buddhist practice and into a form of psychotherapy.

MBSR (Kabat-Zinn, 1990) and MBCT (Segal et al., 2002) employ the psychological principles of stress and coping (e.g. Lazarus & Folkman, 1984) to show how psychological suffering will often emerge in modern life when there is a perceived threat to the self. This may be as a result of social situations where we are in conflict with others or feel excluded by them (Nezlek et al., 2012). It can also be due to life events that challenge our sense of who we are, such as moving house, experiencing a bereavement, going for a job interview, starting a new job, ending or starting a new relationship (Lucas, 2007). For those experiencing chronic depression, the threat may even be the negative judgement that one makes about oneself. Whilst these situations are not life-threatening in themselves, they can still trigger a physiological fight, flight or freeze reaction within us that raises our heartbeat, increases the circulation to our muscles and narrows our attentional focus exclusively to deal with the perceived threat. Over time, such stress reactions can be physically and psychologically debilitating and the cause of further anxiety and distress. According to MBSR and MBCT, it is our difficulty in reconciling these innate alarm reactions with the largely benign nature of our everyday lives that lies at the heart of the modern psychological dilemma in developed nations (Kabat-Zinn, 1990; Segal et al., 2002).

Mindfulness practice (as taught within MBSR and MBCT) encourages participants to recognise the physical aspects of their stress as significant in themselves. This can allow stress reactions to be examined with some psychological distance so that 'real' distress can be differentiated from one's reaction to it in the form of thoughts or actions. Just observing one's reaction with mindfulness can allow habitual, unconscious and automatic stress reactions to be identified and set aside without the need to overthink or act upon them. This can allow an uncoupling of the sensory components of stress from their cognitive and affective counterparts (Kabat-Zinn, 1982).

Mindfulness encourages participants to take a very different relationship to their own thoughts during practice, treating them as transient mental events that come and go in awareness, operating as distractions rather than something to identify with, fixate or act upon. Standing apart from one's thoughts in this way or *decentring* (Sauer & Baer, 2010) allows habitual thoughts to enter consciousness without their usual imperative nature. This is particularly emphasised in MBCT which uses cognitive behavioural theory to show how mindfulness can address chronic depression by interrupting depressive thought processes (Segal et al., 2002). Chronic depression is characterised by rumination: persistent cycles of automatic negatively biased thinking that become increasingly judgmental and self-critical. Ultimately, this can undermine self-worth and lead to a negative view of oneself, the world and the future—a pervasive sense that life is pointless (Beck, 1979). Historically CBT has attempted to correct this kind of 'maladaptive' thinking with approaches such as cognitive restructuring (Clark, 2013) whereby faulty cognitions are identified, evaluated and corrected through rational dialogue with a therapist. Whilst acknowledging similar cognitive dimensions to depression, MBCT does not view rational problem solving (what it refers to as the 'doing' mode) as the road to salvation. Instead, MBCT encourages the direct experience of feelings in the present moment (what it refers to as the 'being' mode) and the suspension of cognitive involvement as a release from depressive rumination (Segal et al., 2002). In essence, applying the same non-judgmental awareness that underpins MBSR.

MBSR and MBCT also suggest that the coping strategies we readily employ to relieve stress, anxiety and depression can often be unconscious and counterproductive. When we have had a particularly difficult time, we may try to suppress the feelings we have by denying their existence or we may turn to alcohol, drugs or food to assuage them. We may even attempt to avoid particular people or situations to negate the appearance of such feelings in the first place. Each of these coping strategies only serves to undermine our ability to cope with the original situation introducing another layer of psychological difficulty into our lives. These self-defeating or maladaptive coping strategies are reinforced over time and become solidified as part of our habitual behaviour. Mindfulness offers an alternative way of coping that can help to recognise and undo some of these unconscious habits.

MBCT and MBSR suggest that participants enlist mindfulness at times of difficulty with a view to accepting the feelings that come up without resorting to their usual compulsions to act or think in certain ways. In this way, mindfulness has "a universal effect of deautomatization, a process in which one's previously established tendency to effortlessly and unconsciously engage in maladaptive behaviors become conscious and controlled" (Kang et al., 2014, p. 168).

Applying Mindfulness to the Digital Domain

Mindfulness and digital interactions appear to be antithetical when it comes to their effects on attention: mindfulness encourages greater attentional control, whilst certain forms of digital interaction can dissipate and overwhelm attentional resources (Ralph et al., 2014). It is easy to see how mindfulness could be useful in addressing the stress, anxiety and depression that comes with increasing digital dependency. However, its value is also immediately apparent when it comes to dealing with the unconscious automatic behaviours relating to digital dependency (e.g. Olson et al., 2020). Digital dependency is characterised by unquestionable 'bad habits' that form over time in relation to digital devices (Bayer & LaRose, 2018) where they become part and parcel of everyday life without us even realising it. Think for instance of the constant checking of smartphones that comes with heavy involvement in social media.

Habits are another important way that we manage attentional control in taxing environments where we establish behaviours as automatic and unconscious thanks to their repetition and reinforcement in relation to particular stable contexts (Orbell & Verplanken, 2010). Digital habits start to form whenever we repeatedly encounter situations where the use of digital technology is necessary or relevant in some way. Given the widespread use of digital technology in developed societies, these kinds of situations are now commonplace. Digital contexts are numerous, multi-faceted, idiosyncratic and at times ambiguous. Digital habits are partly defined by the purpose of an activity itself (e.g. using an online map to find directions somewhere) but also by its relationship to other activities (e.g. whilst getting off a bus in a new town), the social situation (e.g. being in the presence of strangers) or the mood that we are experiencing at the time (such as a sense of urgency or anticipation).

In modern life, digital habits are necessary for maintaining our well-being as they allow us to be productive in our use of digital technology whilst conserving cognitive resources: we do not need to consciously relearn all the steps involved in sending an email or buying online groceries every time we do it. Through repetition, we learn these steps so well that we do not need to actively remember them anymore. They become automatic routines that require minimal conscious awareness to complete, freeing up memory and attentional resources (Garaialde et al., 2020). Digital habits start to become more intrusive and problematic when the purpose of our interaction with digital technology is less clear but habitualised nonetheless. Digital activities such as posting to social media, scrolling through newsfeeds, checking friends' profiles, exploring virtual worlds, playing video games or watching online videos, start life as deliberate acts of techno-social curiosity (Karapanos et al., 2009). We continue to engage in them beyond the novelty stage because we enjoy the social and self-soothing effects that come through them. However, these are open-ended activities and by their very nature, they do not have clear objectives or declared aims. The contexts that drive these kinds of interactions are social and emotional rather than task-based, and this engages a different set of attentional resources that are better suited to open-ended environments but less available to conscious awareness (McGilchrist, 2019; Prabhakaran & Gray, 2012). Whilst repeated use of digital interfaces as part of one's daily routine establishes these activities as automatic routines, over time it is the socio-emotional context itself that becomes the trigger for digital engagement and as attentional demand increases, this invites even greater degrees of unconsciousness (Garaialde et al., 2020). Social situations (such as being alone or being with strangers) and internal psychological states (such as boredom, loneliness or anxiety) can start to provide the cues for digital engagement, and this means that not only is the digital activity automatic but even the initial impetus to engage in it is possibly unavailable to consciousness. As we saw in the previous chapter, it is this heady mix of socio-emotional triggers and the specific affordances of digital technology that create perfect opportunities for exploiting innate human vulnerabilities with expectations for multitasking (Parry & le Roux, 2019) and digital persuasion by design (e.g. Fogg, 2003) increasing the tendency towards unconscious or mindless interaction.

From the perspective of MBCT or MBSR, these mindless digital habits can be seen to operate as avoidant (and maladaptive) coping strategies, providing opportunities to avoid difficult thoughts and emotions relating to situations in the real world rather than engaging with them (Turkle, 2017). Texting a friend during an argument becomes preferable to dealing with them face to face (Turkle, 2017), connecting with friends on social media assuages feelings of loneliness (Seepersad, 2004), and escaping into a video game becomes a way to avoid the stress of everyday life (Kardefelt-Winther, 2014; Koban et al., 2021) or an emotional respite from traumatic life events (Iacovides & Mekler, 2019). Digital technologies provide the perfect way to transfer attention away from any difficult thoughts or feelings we may be experiencing in our immediate situation.

Over time, these unconscious digital habits can create conditions that undermine our general ability to resolve psychological difficulties. Sleep for instance plays an essential role in maintaining psychological equilibrium and is negatively affected by compulsive use. Research consistently shows that compulsive digital interactions interfere with sleep duration and quality. This is the case for general internet use (Alimoradi et al., 2019), social media (Alonzo et al., 2019) and gaming (Wang et al., 2021).

Sleep is responsible for a number of neurophysiological changes that are critical to maintaining our cognitive and emotional wellbeing (Walker, 2009). Without good quality sleep, we become less able to retain positive memories (Walker, 2009) and our attentional capacity starts to dwindle (Whitney et al., 2017). Resolving psychological difficulties becomes harder as we become more fatigued and irritable and our thinking style becomes more negative (Cox et al., 2018). Ultimately, the quality of our social relationships is likely to suffer as well (Kiken et al., 2015).

The nature of specific digital interactions and content can also play into this downward spiral of unconscious (and unhelpful) digital habits with abundant opportunities for indulging negative emotional states online. Social media for instance can provide fuel for depressive rumination (Macrynikola & Miranda, 2019; Parris et al., 2020) and mechanisms that amplify negative emotional states through upward social comparisons (Chou & Edge, 2012), algorithmic control (Wells et al., 2021) and 'doomscrolling' (Sharma et al., 2022).

The Effect of Mindfulness on Unconscious Digital Habits

In theory, mindfulness should be able to help digital users to become more aware of their unconscious digital habits and develop a degree of detachment and attentional control over them, decoupling difficult emotional contexts from the unconscious digital compulsions that arise within them. There is some evidence that those who are naturally more mindful (i.e. high in trait mindfulness) are less prone to this kind of automaticity when it comes to mobile phone text messaging (Bayer et al., 2016) and social media use (Jones et al., 2022). Trait mindfulness also appears to insulate digital users from the depression and anxiety associated with their digital dependencies (Jones et al., 2022; Yang et al., 2019). However, this research is limited in terms of what it can say about the value of mindfulness *training*. Intentional states of mindfulness developed through practice appear to operate independently of any innate capacities for awareness (Kiken et al., 2015) and this makes them more useful when thinking about how to address digital habits and dependencies.

One recent study showed that MBSR training could reduce habitual use of smartphones, online vigilance (the continual devotion of part of one's conscious awareness to the digital realm) and multitasking (Hefner & Freytag, 2021). This small-scale survey suggested that states of mindfulness were beneficial in a number of ways: they made digital users more aware of their habitual online behaviours and the thought patterns that accompanied them. States of mindfulness also operated as 'distraction preventers' (Dunne et al., 2019), helping digital users to resist the attentional demands of multitasking inherent in digital environments. This suggests that it may indeed be possible to leverage the therapeutic effects of mindfulness in relation to digital dependency. However, the quantitative nature of this study makes it difficult to ascertain just how the states of mindfulness changed immediate digital experience and the enactment of unconscious digital habits.

Whilst early research on the relationship between mindfulness and digital wellbeing is encouraging, there is still much we do not know about how mindfulness plays out in the digital realm. In particular, we lack any sense of how digital users experience mindfulness as part of their digital involvement, how it plays out in relation to specific online spaces or digital activities, how it supports the resolution of unhelpful digital habits and whether it leads to greater attentional control over digital interactions. Beyond this, we do not know how those developing their own approaches to digital mindfulness start to renegotiate their engagement with the digital world. Whether they choose to remove themselves entirely from digital demands or to develop greater discernment and deliberation as part of their ongoing digital involvement. These questions demand closer examination and will be pursued further throughout the rest of this book.

Conclusions

This chapter has outlined the basic therapeutic approaches to mindfulness currently in use for chronic pain, stress, anxiety and depression. Mindfulness practice has proven its value in terms of addressing maladaptive coping strategies and this suggests that it may be beneficial in addressing the attentional problems of digital dependency. The following chapter explores this further by considering how those practising mindfulness reconcile this with their digital life through a series of qualitative interviews.

References

Alonzo, R. T., Hussain, J., Anderson, K., & Stranges, S. (2019, December). Interplay between social media use, sleep quality and mental health outcomes in youth: A systematic review. *Sleep Medicine, 64*, S365.

Alimoradi, Z., Lin, C. Y., Broström, A., Bülow, P. H., Bajalan, Z., Griffiths, M. D., ... & Pakpour, A. H. (2019). Internet addiction and sleep problems: A systematic review and meta-analysis. *Sleep Medicine Reviews, 47*, 51–61.

Bayer, J. B., & LaRose, R. (2018). Technology habits: Progress, problems, and prospects. In B. Verplanken (Ed.), *The psychology of habit: Theory, mechanisms, change, and contexts* (pp. 111–130). Springer.

Bayer, J. B., Dal Cin, S., Campbell, S. W., & Panek, E. (2016). Consciousness and self-regulation in mobile communication. *Human Communication Research, 42*(1), 71–97.

Beck, A. T. (Ed.). (1979). *Cognitive therapy of depression.* Guilford press.

Bishop, S. R., Lau, M., Shapiro, S., Carlson, L., Anderson, N. D., Carmody, J., & Devins, G. (2004). Mindfulness: A proposed operational definition. *Clinical Psychology: Science and Practice, 11*(3), 230.

Bodhi, B. (2011). What does mindfulness really mean? *A Canonical Perspective, Contemporary Buddhism, 12*(1), 19–39.

Brewer, J. A., Sinha, R., Chen, J. A., Michalsen, R. N., Babuscio, T. A., Nich, C., ... & Rounsaville, B. J. (2009). Mindfulness training and stress reactivity in substance abuse: Results from a randomized, controlled stage I pilot study. *Substance Abuse, 30*(4), 306–317.

Chou, H. T. G., & Edge, N. (2012). "They are happier and having better lives than I am": The impact of using Facebook on perceptions of others' lives. *Cyberpsychology, Behavior, and Social Networking, 15*(2), 117–121.

Cox, R. C., Cole, D. A., Kramer, E. L., & Olatunji, B. O. (2018). Prospective associations between sleep disturbance and repetitive negative thinking: The mediating roles of focusing and shifting attentional control. *Behavior Therapy, 49*(1), 21–31.

Clark, D. A. (2013). Cognitive restructuring. In S. G. Hofmann & D. Dozois (Eds.), *The Wiley handbook of cognitive behavioral ther-apy*, (pp. 2–22). Wiley-Blackwell.

Dimeff, L., & Linehan, M. M. (2001). Dialectical behavior therapy in a nutshell. *The California Psychologist, 34*(3), 10–13.

Du, J., Kerkhof, P., & van Koningsbruggen, G. M. (2019). Predictors of social media self-control failure: Immediate gratifications, habitual checking, ubiquity, and notifications. *Cyberpsychology, Behavior, and Social Networking, 22*(7), 477–485.

Dunne, J. D., Thompson, E., & Schooler, J. (2019). Mindful meta-awareness: Sustained and non-propositional. *Current Opinion in Psychology, 28*, 307–311.

Fish, J., Brimson, J., & Lynch, S. (2016). Mindfulness interventions delivered by technology without facilitator involvement: What research exists and what are the clinical outcomes? *Mindfulness, 7*(5), 1011–1023.

Fogg, B. J. (2003). *Persuasive Technology: Using Computers to Change What We Think and Do*. Morgan Kaufmann.

Garaialde, D., Bowers, C. P., Pinder, C., Shah, P., Parashar, S., Clark, L., & Cowan, B. R. (2020). Quantifying the impact of making and breaking interface habits. *International Journal of Human-Computer Studies, 142*, 102461.

Gethin, R. (2015). (2015) Buddhist conceptualizations of mindfulness. In K. W. Brown (Ed.), *Handbook of mindfulness: Theory, research, and practice* (pp. 9–41). Ryan RM. The Guilford Press.

Hayes, S. C., Strosahl, K. D., & Wilson, K. G. (2011). *Acceptance and commitment therapy: The process and practice of mindful change*. Guilford Press.

Hefner, D., & Freytag, A. (2021, May). Mindful mobile phone use: A Quasi-experimental study on the effect of Mindful-Based Stress Reduction (MBSR) on Online vigilance, media multitasking, and habitual mobile phone use. The *virtual 71st Annual International Communication Association Conference*, 27–31.

Hofmann, S. G., Sawyer, A. T., Witt, A. A., & Oh, D. (2010). The effect of mindfulness-based therapy on anxiety and depression: A meta-analytic review. *Journal of Consulting and Clinical Psychology, 78*(2), 169.

Iacovides, I., & Mekler. E. D. (2019). The role of gaming during difficult life experiences. *Proceedings of the 2019 CHI Conference on Human Factors in Computing Systems—CHI '19*, 1–12.

Jones, A., Hook, M., Podduturi, P., McKeen, H., Beitzell, E., & Liss, M. (2022). Mindfulness as a mediator in the relationship between social media engagement and depression in young adults. *Personality and Individual Differences, 185*, 111284.

Kabat-Zinn, J. (1982). An outpatient program in behavioral medicine for chronic pain patients based on the practice of mindfulness meditation: Theoretical considerations and preliminary results. *General Hospital Psychiatry, 4*(1), 33–47.

Kabat-Zinn, J., Lipworth, L., & Burney, R. (1985). The clinical use of mindfulness meditation for the self-regulation of chronic pain. *Journal of Behavioral Medicine, 8*(2), 163–190.

Kabat-Zinn, J. (1990). *Full catastrophe living: How to cope with stress, pain and illness using mindfulness meditation*. Bantam Dell.

Kabat-Zinn, J. (1994). *Wherever you go, there you are: Mindfulness meditation in everyday life*. Hyperion.

Kabat-Zinn, J. (2005). *Coming to our senses: Healing ourselves and the world through mindfulness*. Hachette UK.

Kang, Y., Gruber, J., & Gray, J. R. (2014). Deautomatization of cognitive and emotional life. *The Wiley Blackwell Handbook of Mindfulness, 1*, 168.

Karapanos, E., Zimmerman, J., Forlizzi, J., & Martens, J. B. (2009, April). User experience over time: an initial framework. In *Proceedings of the SIGCHI Conference on Human Factors in Computing Systems*, 729–738.

Kardefelt-Winther, D. (2014). The moderating role of psychosocial well-being on the relationship between escapism and excessive online gaming. *Computers in Human Behavior, 38*, 68–74.

Kiken, L. G., Garland, E. L., Bluth, K., Palsson, O. S., & Gaylord, S. A. (2015). From a state to a trait: Trajectories of state mindfulness in meditation during intervention predict changes in trait mindfulness. *Personality and Individual Differences, 81*, 41–46.

Koban, K., Biehl, J., Bornemeier, J., & Ohler, P. (2021). Compensatory video gaming. Gaming behaviours and adverse outcomes and the moderating role of stress, social interaction anxiety, and loneliness. *Behaviour & Information Technology*, 1–18.

Lazarus, R. S., & Folkman, S. (1984). *Stress, appraisal, and coping*. Springer publishing company.

Lucas, R. E. (2007). Adaptation and the set-point model of subjective well-being: Does happiness change after major life events? *Current Directions in Psychological Science, 16*(2), 75–79.

Lukoff, K., Lyngs, U., Gueorguieva, S., Dillman, E. S., Hiniker, A., & Munson, S. A. (2020, July). From Ancient contemplative practice to the app store: Designing a digital container for mindfulness. In *Proceedings of the 2020 ACM Designing Interactive Systems Conference*, 1551–1564.

Lyngs, U., Lukoff, K., Slovak, P., Seymour, W., Webb, H., Jirotka, M., ... & Shadbolt, N. (2020, April). 'I just want to hack myself to not get distracted' evaluating design interventions for self-control on facebook. In *Proceedings of the 2020 CHI Conference on Human Factors in Computing Systems*, 1–15.

Macrynikola, N., & Miranda, R. (2019). Active Facebook use and mood: When digital interaction turns maladaptive. *Computers in Human Behavior, 97*, 271–279.

McGilchrist, I. (2019). *The master and his emissary*. Yale University Press.

Nezlek, J. B., Wesselmann, E. D., Wheeler, L., & Williams, K. D. (2012). Ostracism in everyday life. *Group Dynamics: Theory, Research, and Practice, 16*(2), 91.

Olson, J. A., Stendel, M., & Veissière, S. (2020). Hypnotised by your phone? Smartphone addiction correlates with hypnotisability. *Frontiers in Psychiatry, 11*, 578.

Orbell, S., & Verplanken, B. (2010). The automatic component of habit in health behavior: Habit as cue contingent automaticity. *Health Psychology, 29*(4), 374–383.

Parris, L., Lannin, D. G., Hynes, K., & Yazedjian, A. (2020). Exploring social media rumination: Associations with bullying, cyberbullying, and distress. *Journal of interpersonal violence*. https://journals.sagepub.com/doi/10.1177/0886260520946826

Parry, D. A., & le Roux, D. B. (2019). Media multitasking and cognitive control: A systematic review of interventions. *Computers in Human Behavior, 92*, 316–327.

Prabhakaran, R., & Gray, J. R. (2012). The pervasive nature of unconscious social information processing in executive control. *Frontiers in Human Neuroscience, 6*, 105.

Ralph, B. C., Thomson, D. R., Cheyne, J. A., & Smilek, D. (2014). Media multitasking and failures of attention in everyday life. *Psychological Research Psychologische Forschung, 78*(5), 661–669.

Randolph, P. D., Caldera, Y. M., Tacone, A. M., & Greak, M. L. (1999). The long-term combined effects of medical treatment and a mindfulness-based behavioral program for the multidisciplinary management of chronic pain in west Texas. *Pain Digest, 9*, 103–112.

Rhys Davids, T. W. (1881). *Buddhist Suttas translated from Pāli*. Clarendon Press.

Rhys Davids, T. W., & Rhys Davids, C. A. F. (1910). *Dialogues of the Buddha: Part II*. Henry Frowde.

Sauer, S., & Baer, R. A. (2010). Mindfulness and decentering as mechanisms of change in mindfulness-and acceptance-based interventions. *Assessing mindfulness and acceptance processes in clients: Illuminating the theory and practice of change*, 25–50.

Seepersad, S. (2004). Coping with loneliness: Adolescent online and offline behavior. *CyberPsychology & Behavior, 7*(1), 35–39.

Segal, Z. V., Williams, J. M. G., & Teasdale, J. D. (2002). *Mindfulness-based cognitive therapy for depression: A new approach to preventing relapse*. Guilford Press.

Sharma, B., Lee, S. S., & Johnson, B. K. (2022). The Dark at the End of the Tunnel: Doomscrolling on Social Media Newsfeeds. *Technology, Mind, and Behavior, 3*(1), Spring 2022.

Sriwilai, K., & Charoensukmongkol, P. (2016). Face it, don't Facebook it: Impacts of social media addiction on mindfulness, coping strategies and the consequence on emotional exhaustion. *Stress and Health, 32*(4), 427–434.

Teasdale, J. D., Segal, Z., & Williams, J. M. G. (1995). How does cognitive therapy prevent depressive relapse and why should attentional control (mindfulness) training help? *Behaviour Research and Therapy, 33*(1), 25–39.

Thera, N. (1962). *The heart of Buddhist meditation: A handbook of mental training based on the Buddha's way of mindfulness*. Rider & Co.

Turkle, S. (2017). *Alone together: Why we expect more from technology and less from each other*. Hachette UK.

Walker, M. P. (2009). The role of sleep in cognition and emotion. *Annals of the New York Academy of Sciences, 1156*(1), 168–197.

Wang, Q., Mati, K., & Cai, Y. (2021). The link between problematic internet use, problematic gaming, and psychological distress: Does sleep quality matter? *BMC Psychiatry, 21*(1), 1–11.

Wells, G., Horwitz, J., & Seetharaman, D. (2021). Facebook knows Instagram is toxic for teen girls, company documents show. *The Wall Street Journal*.

Whitney, P., Hinson, J. M., Satterfield, B. C., Grant, D. A., Honn, K. A., & Van Dongen, H. (2017). Sleep deprivation diminishes attentional control effectiveness and impairs flexible adaptation to changing conditions. *Scientific Reports, 7*(1), 1–9.

Williams, M., & Penman, D. (2011). *Mindfulness: A practical guide to finding peace in a frantic world*. Hachette UK.

Yang, X., Zhou, Z., Liu, Q., & Fan, C. (2019). Mobile phone addiction and adolescents' anxiety and depression: The moderating role of mindfulness. *Journal of Child and Family Studies, 28*(3), 822–830.

3

A Qualitative Study of Mindfulness and Digital Practice

Abstract This chapter reports on sixteen qualitative interviews conducted with those who are simultaneously engaged in both regular mindfulness practice and the use of digital technology. These in-depth interviews capture participants' lived experiences and thematic analysis is used to identify three core elements that reflect their progress towards integrating mindfulness practice into their digital lives. These are: (1) an understanding of mindfulness principles; (2) digital self-awareness and (3) techniques for encouraging digital mindfulness. A number of specific issues are identified that characterise the personal dilemmas, negotiations and adaptations pertinent to resolving mindful and digital ways of being. The analysis clearly shows the beneficial effects of mindfulness practice but also highlights the specific difficulties associated with mindless states of digital interaction.

Keywords Qualitative interviews · Mindfulness practice · Hermeneutic phenomenology · Zen · Thematic analysis · Social media · Digital self-awareness · Digital autopilot · Digital mindlessness · Digital rumination · Algorithmic control · Breathing · Anchoring · Compassion

Introduction

There have been two significant shifts in how we understand and live our everyday life in the twenty-first century: the first being the digital revolution and the second that of mindfulness. Digital technology now underpins much of what we do in developed societies and a digital imperative has come to dictate the speed and attentional focus of our everyday lives. The digital dependency that has emerged in relation to this has had important consequences for how we fulfil our basic needs and manage our psychological wellbeing. It has also become a major source of stress, anxiety and depression. At the same time, mindfulness has become increasingly popular as an antidote to the ill effects of modern living with its use encouraged in many walks of life. Some national governments are even starting to recognise its value as a resource and time-efficient remedy for some of the psychological conditions that plague developed societies (Bristow, 2019; Hyland, 2016), those same protagonists: stress, anxiety and depression.

The appearance of these two cultural perspectives or ways of being at the same moment in history is perhaps not coincidental but their coexistence does bring us to a particular dilemma posed by this book: are these two ways of being even compatible? The study contained in this chapter and the following one attempts to answer this and related questions by talking to those who are simultaneously engaged in both ways of being—the digital and the mindful. Qualitative interviews with mindfulness practitioners were used to explore the relationship between digital living and mindfulness. These interviews asked whether digital and mindful practices were complementary or counterproductive and considered how mindfulness practitioners went about resolving these potential contradictions in their everyday lives.

Some would argue that the most reasonable response to this challenge would be to turn our digital devices off and continue without them as they are not compatible with a mindful existence and clearly this is an approach taken by some. The notions of digital abstinence and digital detox have started to gain traction in public discourse with programmes designed to wean people off their digital habits as a way to restore their emotional balance and psychological wellbeing (e.g. Goodin, 2017;

Syvertsen, 2020). Others argue that the benefits of digital connection are too important to discard and suggest that bringing mindfulness to our digital interactions may be a better way to regain control over our lives (Rheingold, 2012). This study engages with this dilemma by considering the experiences of those who are currently engaged in the practice of mindfulness and looks at whether and how the competing demands for attention that arise from digital habits and mindful practice are reconciled in the midst of everyday life.

Methods

To explore the relationship between digital and mindfulness practices, a qualitative interview-based study was conducted with sixteen participants who were simultaneously engaged in both regular mindfulness practice and regular use of digital technology. In order to include a diverse mix of digital and mindfulness experience, participants were recruited through a number of different methods. Initial recruitment took place through the researcher's own university[1] where psychology undergraduates were recruited who were currently involved in mindfulness practice. These participants were self-selecting in response to an email sent out to all Psychology undergraduates, which advertised the study. Many of these participants were under 20 years of age and although they were heavily involved in the digital world, some had limited mindfulness experience in terms of time spent engaged in practice. In order to include participants with greater mindfulness experience, the sample was broadened to include mindfulness tutors and their students who were also older. Mindfulness tutors were contacted directly through their own online recruitment spaces via websites, social media and email. All tutors were teaching a form of mindfulness derived from MBSR and MBCT based approaches. Ultimately eleven mindfulness students and five tutors were interviewed.

---

[1] The University of Brighton in the UK.

Participants

The specific details of all participants are shown in Table 3.1.

Table 3.1 Participants details

Name	Gender	Mindfulness tutor or student	Age group	Mindfulness experience
Gemma	Female	Student	18	Informally online
Fred	Male	Student	20s	Informally online
Nadya	Female	Student	18	Informally online
Almar	Female	Student	18	Informally online
Jack	Male	Student	70s	Formally in person at local Buddhist Centre
Julia	Female	Student	18	Formally as part of mental health support
Holly	Female	Student	18	Formally in person at school
Gloria	Female	Student	20s	Formally in person at school
Rosie	Female	Student	20s	Formally in person at school
Charles	Male	Student	40s	Formally in person at local Buddhist Centre
Ned	Male	Student	60s	Formally in person at local Buddhist Centre
Tara	Female	Teacher	60s	20+ years Buddhist practice and then through secular mindfulness teacher training
Carl	Male	Teacher	50s	30+ years Buddhist practice and then through secular mindfulness teacher training

(continued)

Table 3.1 (continued)

Name	Gender	Mindfulness tutor or student	Age group	Mindfulness experience
Nick	Male	Teacher	40s	20+ years Buddhist practice and then through secular mindfulness teacher training
Sara	Female	Teacher	30s	Learnt mindfulness 2013 via self-help book and later secular mindfulness teacher training
Rachel	Female	Teacher	60s	20+ years Tibetan Buddhist practice and later as secular mindfulness teacher training

Procedure and Context

The interviews were conducted online using video conferencing software (either Microsoft Teams or Zoom) between 9th April 2020 and 23rd November 2021. This period coincided with COVID-19 restrictions and lockdowns in the UK and as such, provided a unique opportunity to investigate the confluence of digital dependency and mindfulness practices. Participants at that time were experiencing an increased dependence on digital connectivity like never before (Sultana et al., 2021) and all mindfulness tutoring was being conducted online. The study received ethical approval from the University of Brighton.

Approach

Semi-structured in-depth interviews were conducted online to explore the lived experience of those practising mindfulness within (and in relation to) digital contexts. The interviews lasted for 35–60 minutes and explored participants' experiences of mindfulness, their specific digital involvements and their views on the compatibility of these different aspects of their life. Through discussion, participants were invited to share the decisions and emotional dilemmas that accompanied their everyday digital involvement and the tactics that they used to maintain their mindfulness in the midst of digital interactions. In addition, the mindfulness tutors were asked about their experiences of teaching mindfulness online.

The approach taken throughout the study was phenomenological with a view to understanding the underlying meanings of lived experience as they related to mindful and digital ways of being. In line with hermeneutic phenomenology (Heidegger et al., 1962), my own pre-understandings of mindfulness and meditation[2] were not set aside but taken as part of the ongoing process of interpretation that informs 'being in the world' (Laverty, 2003). Hence, the interview discussions, analysis and presentation in this book invite a collaborative effort towards understanding digital and mindful ways of being through language, acknowledging the value of subjective understandings. At the same time, any shared or universal sense of 'Being' is recognised as ineffable and unavailable to language, consistent with Zen and Heideggerian philosophies (Storey, 2012).

Analysis

Interviews were transcribed from their digital recordings and 'cleaned up' to aid understanding by removing filler words such as 'ums', 'ahs' and 'kind-ofs'. Analysis of interviews was conducted using thematic analysis (Clarke et al., 2015) which sought to identify common themes that would help to explain how mindfulness and digital ways of being were reconciled.

---

[2] I have been involved in meditation for over thirty years. I started by learning Buddhist practices at a local Buddhist Centre in 1990 and then became involved with Yoga and non-dualist philosophy (e.g. Harding & Smith, 1986; Klein, 1994; Krishnamurti & Cadogan, 1996). Over the last ten years, I have been involved in mindfulness through courses and personal practice.

Initial coding of transcripts was completed using NVivo software in an inductive manner. This revealed a broad range of experiences and interpretations with regard to mindfulness and digital interactions. In making sense of these experiences, I drew upon my own 30+ years of involvement in mindfulness and meditation to inform and clarify themes beyond this point. Three core elements (or latent themes) were developed to reflect participants' progress towards integrating mindfulness practice into their digital lives, (i.e. mindfulness meant different things, the further involved they became with its practices). These provided a simple framework for understanding participants' experiences. For each of the core elements, a number of specific issues (or subthemes) were identified that characterised the personal dilemmas, negotiations and adaptations pertinent to each. Some of these can be accommodated by existing research literature whilst others are novel.

Findings

Integrating Digital and Mindfulness Practices into Everyday Life

Before starting to consider how digital and mindful ways of being come together, it is important to consider how the underlying practices develop in a person's life in the first place. The participants in this study showed varying degrees of experience and 'expertise' when it came to their digital and mindfulness practices, and this was due to their historical learning experiences with both. In relation to mindfulness, it was apparent that the length of time that each had engaged in formal mindfulness practice determined how well they understood the meaning and enactment of mindfulness practice in their everyday lives and this informed an initial framework for understanding mindfulness in a digital world. Three core elements were identified as significant in determining individual experiences of digital mindfulness and progression towards resolving these different ways of being:

1) An understanding of mindfulness principles
2) Digital self-awareness
3) Techniques for encouraging digital mindfulness

Digital practices were similarly affected by prior experience and familiarity but less related to any kind of formal instruction. Here, we explore these elements in turn using them to illustrate some sense of progress in terms of mindfulness practice. In the context of this study, 'progress' should be understood as being supportive of greater psychological wellbeing.

1) An Understanding of Mindfulness Principles

Learning About Mindfulness Online

Four of the younger mindfulness students in the study had learnt about mindfulness solely through the internet, social media and mindfulness apps. As Gemma explained, "[mindfulness] *has been a thing that I've learned about through social media itself*".

Given the possibilities for online misinformation (Anderson & Rainie, 2017) and the alternative interpretations that abound online, it may not be surprising to learn that the knowledge acquired in this way was partial at best. They were often uncertain of where they had first encountered the notion of mindfulness or who they had learnt it from, suggesting that such ideas were just common knowledge.

Gemma explained mindfulness in the following terms, *"it just teaches you to take a step back for a moment and reflect on how you're feeling"*. When asked who she had learnt this from she said, *"it's just stuff that comes up because you've searched for mindfulness, I can't pinpoint anyone specifically"*.

Fred's understanding of mindfulness had come through meditations he had encountered online. As he explained, *"I guess the idea of meditation was probably just from hearing about it, I think, I can't remember exactly how"*. He went on to explain the mindfulness of breathing meditation in the following way: *"I think just focus on your breathing and just sit there for a bit, so yeah, I think that was just from the internet"*.

The 'meme' of mindfulness has become hugely influential with news and popular media, businesses, government departments and celebrities all promoting its value as a panacea for the modern age (Van Dam et al., 2018). Its use is now common in all kinds of contexts from education (Schonert-Reichl & Roeser, 2016) to the workplace (Vonderlin et al., 2020) and even in the military (Purser, 2014). As one might expect, the internet has become a starting point for learning about mindfulness as a concept and a practice. However, the proliferation of mindfulness in online public discourse has led to some divergence in terms of how it is defined and used with an emphasis on simpler practices that are more usefully applicable and immediately beneficial (Purser, 2019). This was apparent in this group of participants.

The lack of formal mindfulness training meant that they were unaware of the significance of certain mindfulness techniques in developing self-awareness. Some were reluctant to engage in practices considered to be essential to MBCT and MBSR. As Gemma explained,

> I'm not really one for the mindful breathing. I find that's not really something that helps me to just control my breathing and think about my breathing. That's not my kind of style.

Within MBCT and MBSR, mindfulness of breathing acts as a gateway activity for engaging with the present moment (Kabat-Zinn, 2012; Williams & Penman, 2011) and for sensitising one to one's own unconscious reactions. It is difficult to see how one could develop mindfulness properly without embracing this experience.

Another participant, Nadya, started using a mindfulness app but confessed that,

> it takes a lot for you to get used to the meditation and to really practice the mindfulness and I didn't have at the time, the patience.

Within the MBCT and MBSR tradition, it is acknowledged from the outset that mindfulness takes time and a commitment to regular practice before the benefits of mindfulness can emerge in relation to one's everyday life (e.g. Kabat-Zinn, 2012; Williams et al., 2007). This is why formal mindfulness courses last for 8–10 weeks long and involve repeated engagement with the 'formal' practices (e.g. the mindfulness of breathing meditations or the body scan) with a view to establishing mindfulness as part of everyday routines. It seems unlikely that mindfulness could be learnt without any commitment to practice.

Specific Misunderstandings of Mindfulness

For those who had learnt about mindfulness online, it was interpreted primarily as a form of relaxation and stress relief, i.e. as a way to avoid the psychological discomfort that may emerge in the present moment. For instance, Almar described her use of the 'Breathe' app[3] on her Apple watch as an example of her engaging with mindfulness,

> it puts you in a room with your mind and you just sit there and kind of think about everything in a positive way and you try to calm down, to slow down.

Similarly, Nadya found her previous experiences of mindfulness practice, learnt from online videos, *"helpful to relax and to kind of destress"*. Such an approach clearly has value in addressing her anxiety but this shows a limited understanding of mindfulness in therapeutic terms (e.g. as defined by MBSR or MBCT). Kabat-Zinn (1990) explains how the motivation to relax can be counterproductive whilst aiming to be aware of one's own body in activities such as the body scan, "if you just work at getting rid of the tension, you may or may not succeed, but you are not practicing mindfulness". Elsewhere, he proposes an inner attitude of "radical acceptance" that will allow one to observe one's own reactions to (physical) suffering with some detachment (Kabat-Zinn, 2005, p. 407).

Whilst there is evidence that online mindfulness resources directed towards self-help can be effective in teaching the basics of mindfulness and reducing anxiety, stress and depression (Cavanagh et al., 2014), the most successful approaches tend to be those that enlist a formal course

---

[3] https://apps.apple.com/us/app/breathe/id1459455352.

structure (Fish et al., 2016). It seems that not all forms of digital mindfulness support are created equal: a recent survey of mindfulness apps identified 370 that were available to download on Google Play. However, when these apps were reviewed by experienced mindfulness teachers, it became evident that many of them overemphasised the use of mindfulness as a form of stress relief (48% of apps), focusing on relaxation (47%) and sleep improvement (29%) and simplifying the overall intent of mindfulness practice (Lukoff et al., 2020).

Digital Mindfulness as Relaxation and Avoidance

What is interesting for this study is how these misunderstandings of mindfulness played out online. For the most part, these participants struggled to see the relevance of mindfulness online. When Fred was asked about how he might enlist mindfulness practice whilst online he just said, *"I'm not sure"*, as if this was an entirely novel concept. Nadya and Almar did not even understand the question. Only Gemma was able to take this a step further saying,

> I think it's just reflecting on how things are making you feel, so if you're online and you think either it could be great and this is really positive and I'm feeling really happy or it's having a negative impact and I should step away from it and do something else, go on a walk.

This seems to suggest the beginnings of some digital self-awareness at an emotional level which could be helpful in developing mindfulness further. However, it is accompanied by an attitude of avoidance with respect to the online world which is unlikely to be beneficial in the long run. Typically, mindfulness encourages an attitude of approach (e.g. Williams & Penman, 2011).

Learning Mindfulness Through Formal In-Person Courses

Eight of the participants in this study had completed formal mindfulness-based courses of 8–10 weeks either at school, through mental health services or through courses run by a local Buddhist Centre. Receiving instruction in this way had encouraged them to have a clearer, more consistent understanding of formal mindfulness practices along with a greater ability to apply mindfulness techniques in their everyday lives. In contrast to the informal group, these participants clearly identified the ways that mindfulness had helped them to deal with their digital life differently, as described here.

Helping Them to Slow Down and Become More Deliberate

Mindfulness practice brought an appreciation of the present moment so that participants were less driven to constantly engage with the next thing that they had to do whilst they were online. As Holly explained, the effects of her mindfulness practice were that, *"you start to slow down a little bit and you start to think OK, why am I doing this, why is this happening?"*.

Encouraging More Conscious Awareness and Self-Control

Other participants found that mindfulness had brought a greater awareness of their 'automatic' reactions to digital situations, allowing them to pause for thought and choose a different, more deliberate course of action. As Jack explained,

> I have more of a conscious awareness of how I'm acting and I find myself being able to intervene. Whilst some of my thoughts might take me in one direction, I do feel that I've got more of a conscious ability to intervene quite quickly and control myself a bit more.

Increasing Emotional Awareness and Regulation

Learning to stay in touch with immediate experience even when it may be uncomfortable had also encouraged a shift in coping strategies from those based on avoidance to those based on approach. As Holly put it,

> It helps you as well with engaging with your own emotions and how you feel towards things so beforehand if I felt a certain emotion to a certain thing, I would just ignore it whereas now I'm like 'OK this is how I'm feeling' and then I carry on. I think it helps me pick out more details and stuff about my life.

Treating Thoughts as Mental Events

Mindfulness practice had also encouraged some participants to maintain a healthy distance from their own thoughts so that they were able to experience emotions as transient sensations rather than mental imperatives. As Rosie explained,

> I can notice when my thoughts aren't making sense so I can sit there and be like no don't take this out on anyone, this isn't you, this is just your emotions and they'll fade away. So having some kind of distance from your thought process and your actions.

Increasing Social Awareness

The awareness developed through mindfulness practice also became evident in social situations.

> It [mindfulness] makes me very present in conversations…I always make sure that I'm thinking about the conversation, I'm not doing anything else. I think it helps with that. My relationships with people and my communication with people—because I'm in the moment and I don't have exterior thoughts or other motives, it's just that conversation. What can I give? What can the person give? Gloria

These reported experiences fit with those one would expect to be learnt and integrated into everyday practice as a result of an MBSR or MBCT course. They reflect many of the characteristics of mindfulness defined by Williams and Penman (2011) and indicate an ability to shift from 'doing' to 'being' mode as part of their mindfulness practice.

2) Digital Self-Awareness

Waking Up to the Digital Autopilot

Those who had learnt about mindfulness through formal in-person courses were much clearer about the effect that mindfulness had on their digital interactions. They had developed a degree of digital self-awareness and were sensitive to the physical, emotional and psychological states that accompanied their digital interactions. They were particularly attuned to the negative states that emerged and attempted to address these by using a mindfulness tactic which is sometimes referred to as "waking up to the automatic pilot" (Kabat-Zinn, 1990; Williams & Penman, 2011). This is a tactic employed during mindfulness training which sensitises students to the automatic and negative patterns that may drive unconscious stress reactions or maladaptive coping strategies. The experiences which prompted concern in the midst of digital interactions varied, ranging from experiences of stress and anxiety to concerns over a loss of conscious control over their life, addiction and hyper-social dilemmas. Here, we explore these reactions in more detail and show the value of increasing awareness.

Stress and Anxiety

Rosie found that interacting online could make her quite anxious and overexcited even when she was interacting with friends,

> actually, depending on the situation I do get quite anxious, I guess I get quite stressed actually. I think it depends on the tone of the conversation, but I had a conversation with my friend last night and we had a really good chat, sending each other voice recordings and that makes me quite giddy and I'm moving around a lot.

Beyond these friendly interactions, Rosie's stress was experienced in other ways,

> I think the internet is a constant stress…there's always something. There's always some social media platform, there's always some notification going off, some fight, ready to be started.

Part of Rosie's frustrations were to do with her difficulty in feeling properly heard by her friends on social media—something we turn to later in relation to hyper-social dilemmas. However, her ongoing relationship to digital interactions of all kinds carried a high degree of stress. She had started to notice that her ongoing stress reactions were making it harder for her to take proper rest.

> I notice when I'm studying, I'll take a break and I'll go on my phone and then I realise that I'm still taking in information instead of letting myself just chill out for a second and it's just, it's not stopping me from stressing
> Rosie

She also described a behavioural reaction to these scenarios where she would *"start being fiddly"* suggesting that she would get physically agitated.

Julia, also experienced a stressful reaction to being online whilst engaged in live sessions of online learning using Microsoft Teams. Here, she had to simultaneously navigate a number of different online interactions, involving multiple live video-based meetings with a university tutor, alongside the joint manipulation of on-screen documents as part of student collaborations. The inherent demands of multitasking here started to affect her breathing and attentional capacity.

> When I'm doing learning online I feel like it stresses me out a bit more. My breathing gets a bit more erratic and I'm not as focused, and then everything kind of goes and I get distracted and then my breathing quickens and then it ends up giving me headaches and things like that.

Shortness of breath is often a direct result of anxiety in the form of hyperventilation. However, this seemed to also be related to the cognitive demands of multitasking that Julia experienced as part of her live teaching sessions. This is possibly an example of cognitive-motor dual task interference (Leone et al., 2017) where her attempts at multitasking had overwhelmed her attentional resources and started to interfere with executive control of unconscious physiological processes (in this case breathing). There have been previous mentions of how intense online activity can interfere with breathing in the form of email apnea (Stone, 2008), but the relationship to multitasking remains poorly understood. Julia also experienced eye strain and extreme tiredness as a result of her excessive engagement with internet, TV and social media on her phone. As she explained,

> I was tired because I was just sitting and not really actively doing anything, like my brain wasn't being used properly, but I was filling up all my time with this endless cycle of watching TV and doing things on my phone, like staying awake, not getting enough sleep.

Here, Julia shows how the initial displacement of attention through the development of digital habits over time resulted in a displacement of healthy activities such as physical activity and sleep.

Digital Mindlessness (and Being Led by the Algorithm)

One of the most significant insights voiced by many of these participants was in relation to periods of mindlessness they experienced whilst engaged in digital interactions. These were moments where they began to realise that they were no longer in control of their own attention or online activities, having handed them over to some automatic online computational process. Holly described it in this way,

> you can tell there are patterns in your online behaviour that you recognise. I don't know what's the word, like you're kind of in an endless loop.

She elaborated in relation to social media,

> you've just done all of this without thinking about it, and you've just watched it like another video and another video you scrolled past more and more posts and it gets to the point where I'm just, I don't know,

> I guess you just think OK, I've just been scrolling for ages and I've got nothing out of scrolling for ages. I've just been doing it for the sake of it like this is giving me no benefit.

These experiences appear to suggest something like a trance state where the algorithm has taken over control of Holly's attention and conscious control for a period of time. However, there is none of the focused engagement or intrinsic enjoyment that one might expect from the flow states commonly associated with gaming (Klasen et al., 2012) or social media (Pelet et al., 2017). These appear to be much more empty and unsatisfying states of consciousness. Holly suggested that her 'digital trances' could easily last for 3 or 4 h whilst using Netflix, Facebook or Instagram before she started to realise their effects on her. Julia's experiences were similar. This shift towards habitual mindless engagement has important consequences for how the present moment is experienced and how it made them feel about their lives. As Julia explained in relation to her compulsive use of social media and streaming television services,

> I felt like I never did anything with my time, it was always wasteful, there was nothing. There was no product of my time, I couldn't tell anyone what I'd done that day, there was nothing to show.

It seemed that the loss of attentional control and the merging of thought processes with those of digital suggestion led to corresponding feelings of unfulfilling emptiness.

Recognising Digital Mindlessness

As already discussed, mindfulness training is squarely aimed at developing a greater awareness of such moments of unconsciousness: the process previously identified as *waking up to the automatic pilot* (Kabat-Zinn, 1990; Williams & Penman, 2011). Some of these participants were making progress in terms of recognising the indicators of these unconscious digital habits and unfulfilling trance-like states. This awareness emerged through uncomfortable physical sensations, repetitive thought patterns and unpleasant emotions that emerged within digital interactions.

Bodily Discomfort and Dissociation

Both Ned and Charles were aware that prolonged periods of online activity would cause them some kind of bodily discomfort. This would often occur when they had to engage in long online video meetings which involved continual poor posture and resulted in back pain.

Rosie's involvement with social media had become so intense that she had started to recognise detachment from her own body as a source of problems whilst interacting directly with others online,

> it's harder to take in what's going on with your body, especially with quick responses, you know you want to be first in there. That can be quite hard to focus on what's going on in yourself.

Gloria had taken this realisation one step further identifying dissociation from her body as one of the indicators of her 'over-involvement' with social media,

> you can get so consumed when you're on social media. It's like your body is just like a vessel and this is your mind. You're just scrolling and taking in information over and over again.

Bodily dissociation of this kind is also a characteristic of hypnotic and trance-like states where control of the conscious mind is deferred to others (Ludwig, 1983). Whilst trance states can be experienced in relation to all kinds of everyday activities such as listening to music, watching films or driving (Butler, 2004), their occurrence is less documented as part of digital interactions except in the context of compulsive gaming (Guglielmucci et al., 2019).

Overthinking and Digital Rumination

Most digital interactions are achieved through a process of asynchronous curation and consumption of symbolic content. This is true of social media as much as it is for email. As such, these are cognitively intensive forms of communication when compared with face-to-face conversations. The demands of interpreting large amounts of text and visual content as part of reciprocal social exchange can easily lead to information overload.

Jack had started to recognise the largely unconscious way that he dealt with his incoming emails and texts saying that it had become a *"semi-automatic process"* for him. This was due to the potential for information overload with him saying, *"I couldn't handle the amount of email I got without filtering quite a lot of it out".*

Holly experienced information overload through an overemphasis on the content of social media posts and an over-analysis of their meaning. Holly described this issue in the following way,

> I guess it's the same for everything, like all social medias and being on my laptop, on my phone, it just depends. If I reach the point where I think I've been watching too much or thinking, overthinking something I've seen on social media, I'll just take a breath.

For Holly, it was this state of 'overthinking' that she saw as an indicator of her unhealthy involvement with social media. She elaborated further,

> I think it's especially Instagram. If I've been looking at a picture too much, if I've been looking at this account too much or on YouTube if I've been looking at one video and then I've been looking at loads that are similar to it, I think I've realised actually I've been like looking at this stuff for quite a while.

Interestingly, she uses the term 'overthinking' here to describe her preoccupation with certain online content. Within the mindfulness tradition, this term is commonly used in another way (e.g. Williams & Penman, 2011) to describe how habitual thoughts about a situation or predicament get in the way of one's awareness of immediate reality and ability to solve everyday problems. Overthinking (or rumination by another name) is also characteristic of those with depression (Matsumoto & Mochizuki, 2018) who find it difficult to stop thinking about past negative events or disappointments which further compound their depressed state. Whilst there is no suggestion that Holly was depressed, she did recognise that her overthinking was sometimes accompanied by negative emotions that could further drive her compulsive use of social media,

> if I'm looking at a picture and I'm like OK, I'm quite jealous of this. I'm like hang on and then I have to think why I'm feeling like that and I'm like well I'm not really. It's different lifestyles and stuff like that.

What is concerning about Holly's example is that her repetitive thoughts are not just a function of her own mind but are kept in place and reinforced by the social media algorithm which continues to present similar content without any concern for how it might be reinforcing her negative emotions. Gloria also expressed a tendency to fixate on social media content that aroused difficult emotions,

> it makes me feel poor, so my issue is that I'll see someone or a celebrity on holiday, or being able to afford to go out, and that's the negative emotion that I get. I'm thinking why am I in the rain in England?.

In Gloria's case, she had become adept at recognising the problematic emotional reactions she had towards online content as indicators of her unhealthy involvement with social media and as moments to take decisive action.

> I think social media can make people feel really awful, but it's also customisable so that you can see what you want. If something's not making me feel good, I will remove it and I thought I have become good at analysing my emotions towards it.

It seems that digital environments such as social media can introduce another dimension to cognition that transforms the very nature of rumination potentially maintaining and prolonging problematic thought patterns or interactions.

Hyper-Social Dilemmas

Digital environments create new opportunities for establishing and maintaining social relationships. However, the very nature of these *hyper-social* connections is such that they can become a source of social disorientation and peer pressure. Social expectations come to be driven not by human capacities and sensibilities but by technological possibilities and priorities. These can introduce additional cognitive demands adding to the stress and anxiety experienced whilst online.

Instantaneous Expectations and the Digital Imperative

One of the ways that this happens is through the time pressure that emerges in digital environments through what might be called a *digital imperative*. Digital technologies allow almost instantaneous contact and ongoing interactions wherever we are on the planet, whatever the time and with multiple people. Whilst this is an obvious boon to many, it can also create unreasonable expectations for constant availability and instantaneous responsiveness that are difficult to live up to. As Rosie explained, this was a significant reason for her stress and anxiety,

> people think that having a phone means you have to constantly be there, not just for them but for the world as well. If someone texts you and you don't reply within say a couple of hours they are going to be like, why haven't they replied to me when they're probably on their phone.

Despite her misgivings, she still felt compelled to respond as soon as she could,

> I try to respond, not always like ASAP, but pretty much when someone texts me.

Rosie identified these underlying conflicts of interest as problematic for her emotional equilibrium with her wanting to remain attentive to her friends whilst at the same time, be in control of her digital usage. She described her inner conflict in the following way:

> I spend too much time online but it's quite hard to escape really. I don't know how to do it without losing all my friends…I definitely struggle with that because I really won't ignore a text more than like 24 hours even if I don't want to open it. Even if I read the notification, I don't wanna see it and I don't wanna talk about it. I will still open it within 24 hours, you know.

As a mindfulness tutor, Sara also recognised this time pressure as one that translated to work environments as well.

> we don't want to feel that we're letting people down or we're not doing our job properly, so then we want to reply immediately, give people what they want, whatever it is they're asking for.

Here, we see a conflation of peer pressure with the *digital imperative* that comes to us through smartphone and computer notifications and a corresponding loss of conscious control over attention, i.e. the hijacking of the innate social need to belong, reinforced by digital notifications. A feature well understood by psychologists (Whiting & Murdock, 2021) and designers (Andrew et al., 2007).

Unfulfilling Social Contact

Whilst hyper-social contact is instant, it does not always allow for the kind of communication that is emotionally fulfilling as Gloria explained,

> digital technology obviously connects a lot of people. It connects people, but it doesn't necessarily mean that it connects you deeply.

Whilst Gloria would often resort to using FaceTime video calls to support greater depth in her communications, this was not always fruitful:

> It is unfulfilling, that's the thing. I find it hard when you haven't spoken to someone for a long time, so it's very superficial conversation because

you don't know about their everyday life, you can't. I can't hear from her every day. Then when you catch up it does, it feels only superficial.

Overthinking was also a feature of Gloria's online video chats. In situations where online conversations required a deep level of emotional understanding, she found it difficult to interpret body language and eye contact adequately, feeling overwhelmed by the artificial nature of these interactions,

> So, I definitely was overthinking it, my brain was really having to, like, where are you looking? Are you looking at the camera? Are you looking at yourself? So, I found it hard, I know I was thinking about it, I was trying but I don't know how effective it was.

Even digital interactions that appear to be very similar to face to face carry additional cognitive load that can easily overwhelm attentional resources and become a source of stress.

Maintaining Conflicts and Digital Rumination

Another way that digital technologies can distort social relationships is by fixing them in time, storing permanent records of interactions and personal profiles that do not reflect the ephemeral nature of one's existence and interactions over time (i.e. those that we have evolved to expect in our daily lives). These permanent records can serve to maintain arguments and reignite difficult emotions way beyond the time when they would 'normally' have dissipated. Rosie recounts her experience of an online argument which showed this playing out,

> I left at one point, I just left it, I didn't delete it, I was like no, just leave it, don't look back on it, but it keeps coming up on my notifications and other people are replying, you know.

She elaborates further,

arguments I've had, I can look back on messages and then I'll start feeling that anger again… People will say, oh, you can delete this, you can leave, you can do this, but I don't think it's always that simple. You've stated it and it will stay there forever more.

This is another example of how social media algorithms can intervene in normal psychosocial processes, creating digital forms of rumination. Whilst mindfulness may encourage us to treat our thoughts as transient mental events, social media sometimes has other ideas.

3) Techniques for Encouraging Digital Mindfulness

Digital Mindfulness Tactics

Mindfulness practices such as 'waking up to the automatic pilot' encouraged a greater awareness of unhelpful digital habits by sensitising users to the physical, emotional and psychological states that accompanied their digital interactions. This can open up an attentional window and provide an opportunity to reassess digital involvement, allowing digital users to make different decisions about how they focus their attention and spend their time. According to mindfulness doctrine, learning how to make use of this attentional window is an important skill to develop for wellbeing and a sense of personal freedom. Inhabiting the present moment in this way can be transformative, allowing a release from the unquestionable digital habits of daily life and a return to the body as the centre of experience. Deliberate choices can be made that are under one's own control rather than in response to any digital demands. Three distinct ways were identified by which mindfulness could help recapture the present moment, the first was by removing oneself from digital involvement entirely, the second involved taking greater control of digital environments and the third involved reinvesting digital interactions with present moment awareness. Here, we explore how the participants in this study employed each of these tactics and their implications for how we understand ongoing relationships and dependencies with digital technology.

The Value of Digital Disconnection

For those who had identified their unconscious digital habits as problematic, removing themselves from the digital world was often seen as an important way of managing their feelings of anxiety, stress, addiction or unfulfilment. This reflected a view of mindfulness and digital interaction as being incompatible and recognised that the difficult emotions this may evoke could be addressed by disconnecting from the digital world. As Holly suggested,

> just realise what you're doing isn't bringing you anything, so do something else or read or just do anything else other than always being like on something digital because that's what it does for me now.

However, it was not an immediate or straightforward process to drop digital habits. Additional techniques had to be deliberately employed to develop a tolerance for *not* being online. For a start, they had to learn to ignore the notifications that would drag them back into their digital interactions and make a point of enforcing time away from digital interactions until the habitual reactions became less compelling. Holly, for instance, would make a point of removing herself from social media some time before she went to sleep,

> if you're on your phone and social media and stuff, you still need to put it down at least half an hour before to wind down, because otherwise your brain is still working, even if it's just reading something or just literally just taking a couple of minutes just by yourself.

Julia applied similar logic for when she woke up in the morning,

> I definitely don't go on the apps as much as I used to go on them. When I woke up in the morning whereas now I'd rather just kind of collect my thoughts. Maybe go and get a hot drink and just sit there and drink it rather than aimlessly scrolling through my phone, which serves no purpose.

Digital disconnection could also be initiated as a periodic act of will, interrupting the endless consumption of content provided by algorithms. As Holly recounted in relation to the never-ending stream of content available via Netflix,

> we'll watch a couple of videos and then just stop and take a breather. OK I've been sat here now for an hour, I don't need to keep sitting here, I can go and turn my attention to something else, so it just made me more aware.

Certain functionality of the digital devices themselves could also be helpful in reinforcing periods of digital disconnection. Most smartphones and tablet computers now come with a 'Do Not Disturb' mode[4] which disables notifications, and this was used by Julia, Holly and Rosie with great effect.

> I do use 'Do Not Disturb' at night times as well. I turn it on when I'm going to sleep, when I'm in bed. I'll turn 'Do Not Disturb' on even if I'm still sat on my phone. So then all the notifications don't rush through. Yeah, that helps you wind down Rosie.

They also used other proprietary apps that could be used to limit their screen time on specific apps.[5] An additional element to the whole digital disconnection approach was engaging in activities that would revitalise the experience of real life—reading printed books, taking walks, doing exercise, being in nature, doing crafts and spending time with friends and family in the 'real' world.

These deliberate acts to remove the influence of digital interaction entirely were seen as a way to allow greater mindful engagement with life more broadly. The mindfulness tutors involved in this study did not by default advocate digital disconnection in this way but understood that limiting digital involvement could be necessary during the initial phases of learning mindfulness practice as part of an MBCT or MBSR course.

---

[4] https://support.apple.com/en-gb/HT204321.
[5] Holly used the Offtime app https://offtime.app/index.php and Julia used Flora https://flora.appfinca.com/ and Forest https://www.forestapp.cc/.

Taking Control of Digital Spaces

Removing oneself from the digital world is not always a possible or desirable option when so much of our everyday lives depends upon it. Another approach to reconciling digital and mindful ways of being whilst remaining digitally connected was to take greater control of the digital space that they were operating in. This could involve deleting apps from their smartphone if they were too distracting or addictive. As Gloria explained,

> I do find myself sometimes, if I've been on social media for too long, I will take control of it. I delete apps like I got addicted to Tik Tok, I've just deleted it, I haven't got it back and yes, I tried to stay in control.

In situations where social media content was distressing or evoked difficult emotions, control could also involve the curation of content, followers and even online 'friends'. As Rosie explained,

> I have recently unfollowed a lot of people on social media because like influencers and stuff, because that's quite stressful as well for me, just you know, seeing like highly attractive people on holidays, places with expensive clothes, it's too much for me right now.

Taking control could also involve redefining social norms of behaviour so that digital technology was no longer relevant as Gloria described in relation to nights spent with her flatmates,

> we all just put our phones away, we all put our phones next to the TV and we can't touch it. First person that does has to do the recycling or something but normally it's fine, no one wants to even do it.

Gloria was of the view that collective action (both online and offline) was the only way to change the norms of digital behaviour that were responsible for creating stress and anxiety.

Developing Mindfulness in Situ

Perhaps, the most direct application of mindfulness practice encountered during this study was that undertaken by the mindfulness tutors (and some of the students). This reflected a global approach to mindfulness which did not see it as incompatible with digital interactions. As Nick explained,

> mindfulness is about being present in the world so you know, the world has its digital aspect…then there has to be a quality of practising mindfulness in the digital age.

This approach involved bringing present moment awareness to digital experiences and transforming one's inner relationship to these as they were taking place.

Single-Pointed Awareness

A starting point for being digitally mindful in this way was to create the conditions for this quality of interaction. This involved focusing attention exclusively on one digital activity at a time, avoiding multitasking and turning off all notifications and other digital distractions. Tara explained the benefits of removing all of these background distractions,

> that sort of level of multitasking, if that's what it is, is not very supportive for someone who's trying to practise mindfulness.

Indeed, it was important to bust the whole myth of multitasking as Jack described,

> I don't have to go from one thing to another, I don't think there is an actual multitasking. You're going from one thing to another. You might be doing it quite quickly, got it. Even momentarily, your focus is on one thing and then it's on another. I don't think you're doing both.

3 A Qualitative Study of Mindfulness and Digital Practice

Slowing Down and Taking Notice (Curiosity)
The tutors suggested that once digital engagement had been simplified in this way it was important to slow down interactions with the physical device and screen, so that it was possible to notice from moment to moment the sensations that accompanied digital interaction. This involved suspending any tendency to interact at 'digital speed' and slowing this down to a pace that allowed for physical and psychological reactions to be observed (i.e. human speed). As Carl explained in relation to exploring unhelpful digital habits,

> the invitation is always just to try and notice how you're getting drawn into these kind of things so they could be useful.

The suggestion here was *not* to avoid stressful or habitual digital interactions but instead to sit with them and notice how they were affecting you on a psychological, emotional and physical level in the moment; to see how they were actually experienced rather than any idea of what was happening or assumptions about having to conform to digital imperatives. This would widen the attentional window and give some space between thought and digital action to exist. As Nick explained, this allows us to choose how to respond rather than reacting automatically,

> we train in cultivating agency by noticing when the mind has wandered and we bring it back to a chosen anchor so, in the same way we can spot when there's the pull to click on that particular app button yet again when actually it's not serving us and to notice what the sensations are, to notice what the urges are and how that feels and the impulses and actually to bring ourselves into the present with that, so that we've got the possibility of making skilful choices.

Anchoring in Physical Experience
As Nick hinted at in the previous quote, physical sensations could be used to 'anchor' oneself in relation to digital interactions so that one can maintain a presence in immediate human experiential time (Germer, 2005) rather than that prescribed by digital technology. In mindfulness practice, anchors are essential for maintaining a focus on the present

moment and often involve paying close attention to physical sensations. One of the most common anchors used is the immediate physical experience of breathing as Holly described here,

> If I am thinking that if I'm looking at something and it's elicited a bigger emotional response in me, I will just put my phone down and take a couple of breaths to recentre myself and then I either carry on looking at social media or I just stop and I'll do something else.

Being Kind and Compassionate
Whilst all the tutors in this study were involved in teaching secular mindfulness courses online, based on MBSR and MBCT, they had been heavily influenced by early experiences with Buddhist meditation and philosophy. This meant that they had an appreciation of the practices as being inter-relational at their core and incorporated kindness and compassion as essential aspects of mindfulness. Carl explained that whilst digital forms of contact like email and social media were commonly used for *"zoning out"* or *"avoiding"*, at their best they could be used for *"generating kindness and awareness"*.

An emphasis on compassion for other human beings was also evident in the way that they employed digital technologies to teach mindfulness. Tara outlined her concerns about the dehumanisation that could emerge whilst using social media or online forums,

> It's easy to get into dealing with a view or a statement or a concept, and you kind of forget that that's actually a person.

She suggested that slowing down was also an appropriate way of approaching text-based forms of digital interaction so that the sense of the other person was always retained.

> I think there's certainly something about taking time to ponder responses that perhaps is easily squeezed out with social media.

The online mindfulness courses created by all the tutors (including Tara's) were deliberately created to support a high degree of interpersonal awareness, sensitivity to participants and group involvement. During the period of the study, mindfulness classes were typically conducted online using Zoom and the spaces that they created, provided safe environments for their students to explore mindful ways of being online, legitimising the whole notion of mindfulness in the digital world.

Conclusions

This chapter has explored the experiences of those attempting to reconcile mindful and digital ways of being in their everyday lives. Three core elements were identified as important to them in developing as part of this endeavour: (1) an understanding of mindfulness principles; (2) digital self-awareness and (3) techniques for encouraging digital mindfulness. The final chapter relates these findings to the initial concerns highlighted in the book revisiting the relationship between wellbeing and digital dependency and explaining this in terms of a displacement of attention. In addition, it explores the value of mindfulness tactics in addressing these underlying concerns.

References

Anderson, J., & Rainie, L. (2017). The future of truth and misinformation online. *Pew Research Center, 19*.

Andrew, A., Borriello, G., & Fogarty, J. (2007, April). Toward a systematic understanding of suggestion tactics in persuasive technologies. In *International conference on persuasive technology* (pp. 259–270). Springer.

Bristow, J. (2019). Mindfulness in politics and public policy. *Current Opinion in Psychology, 28*, 87–91.

Butler, L. D. (2004). The dissociations of everyday life. *Journal of Trauma & Dissociation, 5*(2), 1–11.

Cavanagh, K., Strauss, C., Forder, L., & Jones, F. (2014). Can mindfulness and acceptance be learnt by self-help?: A systematic review and meta-analysis of mindfulness and acceptance-based self-help interventions. *Clinical Psychology Review, 34*(2), 118–129.

Clarke, V., Braun, V., & Hayfield, N. (2015). Thematic analysis. *Qualitative Psychology: A Practical Guide to Research Methods, 222*(2015), 248.

Fish, J., Brimson, J., & Lynch, S. (2016). Mindfulness interventions delivered by technology without facilitator involvement: What research exists and what are the clinical outcomes? *Mindfulness, 7*(5), 1011–1023.

Germer, C. K. (2005). Teaching mindfulness in therapy. *Mindfulness and Psychotherapy, 1*(2), 113–129.

Goodin, T. (2017). *Off. Your digital detox for a better life*. Hachette UK.

Guglielmucci, F., Monti, M., Franzoi, I. G., Santoro, G., Granieri, A., Billieux, J., & Schimmenti, A. (2019). Dissociation in problematic gaming: A systematic review. *Current Addiction Reports, 6*(1), 1–14.

Harding, D. E., & Smith, H. (1986). *On having no head: Zen and the rediscovery of the obvious* (p. 81). Arkana.

Heidegger, M., Macquarrie, J., & Robinson, E. (1962). *Being and time*. Blackwell Publishers.

Hyland, T. (2016). *Mindful nation UK–report by the mindfulness all-party parliamentary group* (MAPPG).

Kabat-Zinn, J. (1990). *Full catastrophe living: How to cope with stress, pain and illness using mindfulness meditation*. Bantam Dell.

Kabat-Zinn, J. (2005). *Coming to our senses: Healing ourselves and the world through mindfulness*. Hachette UK.

Kabat-Zinn, J. (2012). *Mindfulness for beginners: Reclaiming the present moment—and your life*. Sounds True.

Klasen, M., Weber, R., Kircher, T. T., Mathiak, K. A., & Mathiak, K. (2012). Neural contributions to flow experience during video game playing. *Social Cognitive and Affective Neuroscience, 7*(4), 485–495.

Klein, J. (1994). *Beyond knowledge*. Third Millennium Pubications.

Krishnamurti, J., & Cadogan, M. (1996). *Total freedom: The essential Krishnamurti* (p. 384). HarperSanFrancisco.

Laverty, S. M. (2003). Hermeneutic phenomenology and phenomenology: A comparison of historical and methodological considerations. *International Journal of Qualitative Methods, 2*(3), 21–35.

Leone, C., Feys, P., Moumdjian, L., D'Amico, E., Zappia, M., & Patti, F. (2017). Cognitive-motor dual-task interference: A systematic review of neural correlates. *Neuroscience & Biobehavioral Reviews, 75*, 348–360.

Ludwig, A. M. (1983). The psychobiological functions of dissociation. *American Journal of Clinical Hypnosis, 26*(2), 93–99.

Lukoff, K., Lyngs, U., Gueorguieva, S., Dillman, E. S., Hiniker, A., & Munson, S. A. (2020, July). From ancient contemplative practice to the app store: Designing a digital container for mindfulness. In *Proceedings of the 2020 ACM Designing Interactive Systems Conference*, 1551–1564.

Matsumoto, N., & Mochizuki, S. (2018). Why do people overthink? A longitudinal investigation of a meta-cognitive model and uncontrollability of rumination. *Behavioural and Cognitive Psychotherapy, 46*(4), 504–509.

Pelet, J. É., Ettis, S., & Cowart, K. (2017). Optimal experience of flow enhanced by telepresence: Evidence from social media use. *Information & Management, 54*(1), 115–128.

Purser, R. (2014). The militarization of mindfulness. *Inquiring Mind, Spring*. Retrieved March 28, 2022, available from: https://www.inquiringmind.com/article/3002_17_purser-the-militarization-of-mindfulness/

Purser, R. (2019). *McMindfulness: How mindfulness became the new capitalist spirituality*. Repeater.

Rheingold, H. (2012). *Net smart: How to thrive online*. Mit Press.

Schonert-Reichl, K. A., & Roeser, R. W. (2016). Mindfulness in education: Introduction and overview of the handbook. In *Handbook of mindfulness in education* (pp. 3–16). Springer.

Stone, L. (2008, February 8). *Just Breathe: Building the case for Email Apnea*. Huffington Post. http://www.huffingtonpost.com/linda-stone/just-breathe-building-the_b_85651.html

Storey, D. (2012). Zen in Heidegger's way, Journal of East-West. *Thought, 2*(4), 113–137.

Sultana, A., Tasnim, S., Hossain, M. M., Bhattacharya, S., & Purohit, N. (2021). Digital screen time during the COVID-19 pandemic: A public health concern. *F1000Research, 10*(81), 81.

Syvertsen, T. (2020). *Digital detox: The politics of disconnecting*. Emerald Group Publishing.

Van Dam, N. T., Van Vugt, M. K., Vago, D. R., Schmalzl, L., Saron, C. D., Olendzki, A., & Meyer, D. E. (2018). Mind the hype: A critical evaluation and prescriptive agenda for research on mindfulness and meditation. *Perspectives on Psychological Science, 13*(1), 36–61.

Vonderlin, R., Biermann, M., Bohus, M., & Lyssenko, L. (2020). Mindfulness-based programs in the workplace: A meta-analysis of randomized controlled trials. *Mindfulness, 11*(7), 1579–1598.

Whiting, W. L., & Murdock, K. K. (2021). Notification alert! Effects of auditory text alerts on attention and heart rate variability across three developmental periods. *Quarterly Journal of Experimental Psychology, 74*(11), 1900–1913.

Williams, M., & Penman, D. (2011). *Mindfulness: A practical guide to finding peace in a frantic world*. Hachette UK.

Williams, J. M. G., Teasdale, J. D., Segal, Z. V., & Kabat-Zinn, J. (2007). *The mindful way through depression: Freeing yourself from chronic unhappiness.* Guilford Press.

4

A Digital Approach to Mindfulness

Abstract This chapter provides a detailed discussion of the experiences recounted in Chapter 3, exploring a broader contextual understanding of the mindless states that emerge in relation to digital environments and their effects on attention and wellbeing. Of particular concern, here is the delegation of attentional control that seemed to accompany digital dependency and the potential problem of *digital rumination* in relation to social media algorithms. The challenge for those wishing to become more mindful in a digital world is reduced to three imperatives (the digital, the hyper-real and the algorithmic), all of which drive unconscious forms of interaction and draw users away from the present moment. The chapter concludes with guidelines for dealing with these imperatives, explores the implications they have for Cyberpsychology research and a digital approach to mindfulness practice.

Keywords Wellbeing · Digital rumination · Digital imperative · Algorithm · Hyper-reality · Attentional control · Mindfulness · Guidelines · Government regulation · Attention economy · Zen · COVID-19

Introduction

This book started by highlighting concerns over increasing dependence on digital devices in developed societies and the potentially corrosive effect that this may be having on our psychological functioning and wellbeing. In Chapter 1, it was also posited that the displacement of attention was at the core of this modern dilemma whereby digital interactions are seen as colonising attention at an unconscious level and interfering with normal functioning. The participants of the study in Chapter 3 were deliberately chosen as they were all practising mindfulness (in varying degrees) and this allowed an examination of attentional processes to take place in relation to digital interactions. Now, in this final chapter, these findings are considered in more depth with a view to explaining why attentional disruption occurs and the implications that this may have for Cyberpsychology and mindfulness practice.

The Effects of Digital Interaction on Attention and Wellbeing

The mindfulness students in the previous study all benefited from their involvement in the digital world but they also identified certain kinds of digital interactions as significant and incapacitating sources of stress and anxiety in their everyday lives. These stresses were experienced physically through bodily discomfort, tension, agitation, tiredness, dissociation and breathing problems. In these instances, multitasking, information overload and the instantaneous expectations of digital communication were implicated in overwhelming attentional capacity, driving unconscious forms of interaction and in so doing becoming a source of stress.

Shifts towards dysfunctional and compulsive forms of digital engagement were often accompanied by a delegation of attentional control away from themselves to some form of computational suggestion or control (e.g. the algorithms that suggest content within social or streaming media). The resulting mindless or trance-like states were able to blur the origins of intentionality and maintain engagement for extended periods.

Over time, this led to feelings of dissatisfaction and unfulfilment with negative effects on wellbeing.

There was also the suggestion that content provided by social media algorithms was repetitive and immutable which when combined with this delegation of attentional control could lead to a form of *digital rumination*. Rather than allowing difficult emotions, memories or thoughts to dissipate naturally over time, this merging of computational and human thought processes in this way was likely to prolong negative emotional states and social conflicts.

Recent disclosures from social media companies such as Meta show that social media algorithms attune to and amplify content that is violent, distressing, argumentative or which can reinforce a negative view of the self (Hagey & Horwitz, 2021; Wells et al., 2021). In an attentional sense, it is clear to see how psychological entanglement with such algorithms is likely to drive an increasingly mindless mode of interaction and have negative effects on wellbeing. The participants in this study were fortunate enough to be aware of such effects and this was, in part, due to their involvement in mindfulness.

Applying Mindfulness to Digital Interaction (Explaining the Dilemma)

We are increasingly turning to digital technologies to think and remember things for us and to keep our minds occupied. Consider how we have come to rely on search engines to answer our everyday queries about cooking, trivia or how to mend the car, how we rely on algorithms to choose news, entertainment and books for us, social media to maintain our relationships and online maps to find out where we are and where we are going. This reflects a profound shift in the way that we use our minds, where access to digital information and computational processes has become synonymous with thinking, acting and even being. Digital technologies extend our innate human capabilities (Clark & Chalmers, 1998) in a form of cognitive outsourcing or offloading (Risko & Gilbert, 2016), that allows us to complete tasks or acquire knowledge in ways that were not previously possible. This has implications for how we understand the nature of attention and mindfulness as it signals a shift in emphasis from internal to external web-based processes as the attentional focus in everyday life: where embodied thought was once the originator of action, now web-based suggestions become more likely forms of inspiration or influence. Mindfulness in the digital world therefore becomes about recognising this attentional shift and learning to navigate it in a beneficial way.

As outlined earlier in the book, attention operates differently depending upon the context we are in and how we interpret the nature of each context. At one extreme, we have top-down, conscious, goal-driven attention, which is used for planning and completing tasks, whilst at the other extreme, we have bottom-up, largely unconscious, stimulus-driven attention which gives us an ever-present awareness of our surroundings, operating in the background and giving us the ability to respond to unanticipated environmental changes or events (McGilchrist, 2019). When we engage with digital environments, it therefore matters how we interpret the nature of the space when it comes to understanding its effects on our attention.

Dealing with the Digital Imperative

Historically computer systems were developed to help us complete arduous tasks where the computer would take over memory or calculation functions that we humans were less efficient at. Paying attention to such systems would involve inputting data and issuing relevant commands to make the computer do some calculations. This involved deliberate, conscious attention to activities initiated by the user. Over time, these systems have developed in speed and complexity, taking over more and more of our intimate cognitive activity to the extent that we may wonder who or what is actually in control. As I write this chapter, I am struck by the instructions given to me by the word processing programme to change my spelling and restructure my sentences. Beyond this window of attention are the demands of competing apps telling me what the weather is like outside my own window, giving me snippets of the latest world news (and inviting me to learn more) or notifying me that someone has just started following me on Twitter (and maybe I should follow them?). These are automatic prompts programmed into apps to mimic human responsiveness whilst asserting notions of productivity. Current digital environments demand that we interact with them, that is, they represent a *digital imperative* in our lives. This imperative is driven by a computer-based logic that by necessity transforms everything into overt tasks (including the subtleties of human interaction) and emphasises efficiency in action, communication and societal transactions. It anticipates abilities in multitasking, information capacity and processing speed that far outweigh our human abilities. When we relate to computers in the context of task completion, mindless interaction starts to occur when we assume this digital imperative as our own and our attentional capacity becomes exhausted as a result.

When it comes to engaging in task-based or deliberate activities, computers and digital networks are still incredible tools and we would do well to continue using them. However, our relationship with computers is asymmetrical and we must learn to recognise and acknowledge our own attentional limits as human beings. This study has shown how mindfulness (once established as a regular practice in one's life) can help to do this by sensitising users to the physical aspects of stress and anxiety that accompany attentional exhaustion in relation to digital engagement. Useful approaches encountered during the study are collated below.

Guidelines for Dealing with the Digital Imperative:

1. Periodically shifting your attention back to the body and anchoring yourself in immediate bodily experience provides a means of checking on how your digital engagement is affecting you and of clarifying your own sense of purpose in lieu of digital imperatives.
2. Pausing to become aware of your own breath whilst using digital technology can be helpful, even if this is for a brief moment. This reconnects you with human rather than digital imperatives, providing an opportunity to reassess the quality of your own digital engagement and a chance to decide what to do next (e.g. continue, revise your engagement or take a break from digital technology).

3. You can take pragmatic steps to reduce the attentional demands of your digital engagement whenever you feel that your attentional capacity is being overwhelmed. This can be done by limiting multi-tasking by closing down all devices/windows/apps other than the one you are currently working with; turning off notifications from all other apps and taking greater control of the digital space that you are working within by curating content that is helpful rather than distracting.

Given that computers and digital networks are now part and parcel of most people's working lives and the administrative tasks of everyday life, these suggestions would be helpful in managing the attentional demands of task completion at a conscious level. However, there are other developments which further complicate our involvement with digital technology and push us towards greater mindless forms of interaction.

Dealing with the Hyper-Real (and Algorithmic) Imperatives

The advent of the internet and World Wide Web saw a shift in the way that computers were used from one designed for explicit task completion to one that was also concerned with the elaboration of human communication and connection en masse. Digital spaces have increasingly become "third places" (Oldenburg, 1999) where we meet, connect and socialise with others; this has signalled a shift from 'doing' things with digital technology to 'being' in digital spaces where we are expected to invest more of ourselves in the process of digital presentation and social interaction. In this context, it appears to be bottom-up, stimulus-driven forms of attention that have become more significant.

What drives mindlessness or unconscious reactions here, originates in a form of super stimulation that is now accepted practice online and which taps into our evolutionary heritage in ways that we find difficult to ignore or manage. Most forms of internet-enabled interaction from web searching to using online forums or social media, watching videos on streaming media, playing video games or interacting through virtual worlds, present us with experiences that we are hard-wired to pay attention to, but which surpass anything that we would normally encounter in 'real' life. This is true in terms of the unprecedented instant access they give us to content that is novel, informative, entertaining, provocative, misleading or threatening. It is also present in the unique way that they allow us to relate to others, amplifying and distorting processes of self-presentation, affiliation and social interaction. It is here that the potential for mindlessness can emerge through a digital outsourcing of self-knowledge where the processes of self-reflection start to become automated.

In order to establish a meaningful online presence (especially in the public 'open' spaces of the internet), it is necessary to commit oneself to an escalating arms race for attention where one projects oneself into the digital world (broadcasting to a seemingly infinite audience) in ways that are endlessly appealing, shocking or idealised. This was particularly an issue for the younger participants in the study who were heavily involved in social media but clearly part of everyone's online experience. Using CAPITAL LETTERS in emails, phrasing tweets in a provocative, pithy manner or using filters on Instagram to get more likes and followers are all part of the new vocabulary of self-promotion that typifies the current culture of the internet where gaining attention is of paramount importance (even if we choose not to take part in it, we will be aware of it). App and social media profiles must be constantly reviewed and updated to maintain one's online presence in this hyper-reality where one's posts to assumed audiences and their reactions to them become a source for autobiographical memory and self-knowledge (Wang et al., 2017). When digital interactions become habitual, identification with the online persona increases, distinctions between the real and digital self become blurred and digital involvement is experienced as compulsive and a matter of life and death (Harley, 2019).

The heightened nature of such environments can stretch the limits of attentional capacity and start to push one towards greater mindlessness where unconscious reactions to others start to predominate in the form of negativity bias (Lang et al., 2007; Park, 2015) and one becomes sensitised towards unpleasant emotions, feelings of threat and discord. In such saturated environments, it is bottom-up, stimulus-driven forms of attention that start to kick in. However, there is another layer to this relationship which can further complicate our understanding of underlying shifts in attention. The interactions that take place with others online are not as transparent as they may appear: there are other influences at play that distort these interactions in unhelpful ways. Developing alongside this hyper-reality is an advertising model that views our attention as a commodity (Zuboff, 2019). Internet algorithms (i.e. those present in web search, streaming and social media) are designed to learn what content users pay most attention to, and then to present similar or related content back to them in order to keep hold of their attention. The prioritisation of content is driven by incidental personal data as much as it is by deliberate consumption choices (Kozyreva et al., 2021). Unfortunately, these algorithms serve to amplify unconscious human tendencies towards paying attention to extreme emotional states. Whilst the algorithm is essentially agnostic with regard to which emotions get amplified, it is feelings of threat and discord that appear to be most contagious (Bradley et al., 2007; Hagey & Horowitz, 2021).

The previous study has shown how algorithms can reinforce negative social comparisons that lead to persistent feelings of envy, jealousy and unresolved conflict that are difficult to manage. This can result in a form of *digital rumination* where persistent negative thoughts are temporarily mistaken for one's own when they are in fact being delivered to consciousness by an algorithm. From a mindfulness perspective, it is the delegation of attentional control to computational processes that is significant here. Whilst not reported as part of this study, it is highly likely that a similar delegation of attentional control occurs in relation to positive emotional states (Goldenberg & Gross, 2020) and whilst this may appear unproblematic, it would clearly help to kick-start a mindless relationship with social media that can easily turn sour once different unconscious biases start to get amplified by the algorithm.

Mindless interactions start to occur when there is an over-identification with the digital self (as part of involvement in a hyper-reality) and a delegation of attentional control to an algorithmic imperative which is ultimately driven by a profit motive rather than one concerned for (one's own) psychological wellbeing.

As we saw with the digital imperative, there is a pervasive trend towards mindlessness that is built into current forms of digital interaction where our attention and behaviour are driven by ideals of technological efficiency (the digital imperative), economic gain (the algorithmic imperative) and the social norms of internet-based interactions (the hyper-real imperative). In the midst of such competing demands, it is important to come back to one's own *human* imperative (which may even be no imperative). Mindfulness can be helpful in enabling this reorientation to take place and suggestions from the study are collated below.

Guidelines for Dealing with Hyper-Reality and Algorithmic Imperatives:

1. Ensure you have periods of digital disconnection where all devices are switched off. This is necessary for acquainting yourself with your own thought processes and emotional states. Learn to differentiate your own thoughts and emotions from those provoked by extreme digital interactions (hyper-reality) as well as the algorithm's computerised substitutions for thought.
2. Practice mindfulness whilst engaging in digital interactions.
    - Maintain single-pointed awareness where possible, e.g. interact with one person or known group of people at a time.
    - Slow down and take notice of how digital interactions make you feel—remember to go at human speed when you can.
    - Be kind and compassionate—remember that digital interactions involve other people.
3. Take control of digital spaces by asserting the importance of connections with 'real' friends and congruence with your offline self. Challenge the assumptions of hyper-reality and make this a socially relevant issue—discuss with your friends, colleagues and family what the most beneficial ways are for you to behave in relation to digital technology.

Implications for Cyberpsychology

Digital technology is now part of everyday life for the majority of people living in developed nations. It is no longer easy to live your life without it and its influence is felt everywhere. Rather than passing judgement on the pervasiveness of digital technology, this book has tried to explore how to go about maintaining a beneficial relationship with it so that we can protect our psychological wellbeing and continue to thrive in a digital world.

The Displacement of Attention Versus the Displacement of Behaviour

This book proposed an approach to understanding dysfunctional relationships with digital technology in terms of displacements of attention rather than behaviour. Viewing digital interactions in this way has shown that shifts towards greater unconsciousness or mindlessness are important indicators of dysfunctional and compulsive use. From a user's perspective, this means that gaining a greater appreciation of how one employs one's own attention is likely to be a fruitful way to address digital dependencies. It has also shown that these shifts towards mindlessness are not the sole responsibility of users but are often due to other forces at play in digital environments, namely the imperatives of digital technologies, algorithms and the social norms of hyper-reality. A more complete assertion would be that the displacement of attention occurs because of a delegation of attentional control to these external imperatives. Observing this fact can serve to de-pathologise the notion of digital dependency and reinvigorate a sense of agency for digital users.

In line with original use of the term 'displacement' in psychology (e.g. Freud, 1905), it was also deemed important to gain an understanding of the underlying causes for the displacement of attention. Previous studies on internet addiction have suggested that the displacement of behaviour (e.g. physical or face to face social activities) occurs as a form of psychological defence or coping mechanism, where the internet is used as an escape from stressful circumstances elsewhere in a person's life (e.g. Kardefelt-Winther, 2014). This study has shown that the compulsion to interact digitally can also be understood through a delegation of attentional control to computers in line with the extended mind thesis (Clark & Chalmers, 1998). This suggests that a displacement of attention can occur as a direct result of the attentional demands of digital environments. Again, this points to digital environments themselves as being a source of dependency, stress, anxiety, emotional discomfort and unfulfilment rather than the user.

The Need for the Regulation of Online Behaviour and Algorithms

There is now greater understanding and acknowledgement of the impact of social media on wellbeing with psychological research showing vulnerabilities in terms of age, personality and underlying motivations for use (Dailey et al., 2020; Kircaburun et al., 2020). Recent disclosures at Meta have also shown that social media algorithms can be responsible for increasing stress, anxiety, sadness, loneliness and body image concerns amongst teenage users of their apps (Hagey & Horwitz, 2021; Wells et al., 2021). Without some form of regulation, it is likely that the extremes of online behaviour and the exaggerating influence of algorithms will continue unabated. We also know that algorithms and other forms of AI are increasingly being employed as guiding principles within emerging technologies from job-hiring algorithms to care robots to self-driving cars (Elliott, 2019). These technologies will require similar scrutiny with regard to how their algorithms affect attention and wellbeing.

Fortunately, there are organisations such as the Center for Humane Technology (https://www.humanetech.com/) who are leading the way in terms of highlighting ethical concerns about this new *attention economy*, with proposals for policy reform and redesign of digital platforms. National governments have been slow to realise the impact of these technologies and we are only now seeing an approach to regulating aspects of hyper-reality and the algorithms that operate in this space (e.g. Australian Government, 2021; European Commission, 2020; UK

Government, 2021). These proposed forms of regulation will hold digital platforms and social media companies accountable for any illegal or 'legal but harmful' (UK Government, 2021) content, imposing fines when it is allowed to circulate on their sites. This is certainly a good start in terms of dealing with the 'bad actors' and criminality of hyper-reality but may struggle to address the full breadth of harmful content which will be open to interpretation by a regulator, and may risk undermining freedom of expression online (Trengove et al., 2022). From the perspective of mindfulness, this legislation is currently lacking in terms of recognising the systemic issues within digital platforms and social media that adversely affect attention and wellbeing. The unconscious manipulation of users through algorithmic control is notoriously covert and there needs to be much greater transparency about how this operates within digital environments. Only the European legislation is currently sophisticated enough to address this through the use of algorithm audits (European Commission, 2020). Even better would be a requirement on digital platforms to make their algorithmic controls transparent to the user. Learning to differentiate human from computerised thought will become an important skill if we want to thrive in a future digital world. All the while this influence remains hidden, it will be harder to recognise the negative effects of algorithmic influence.

Implications for Mindfulness Training

This study has shown that mindfulness has an important role to play in maintaining beneficial relationships with digital technology. It has also revealed the particular challenges that digital technology represents for those learning mindfulness for the first time. Three core elements were identified as important to develop as part of exploring a digital approach to mindfulness and these could be easily integrated into teaching sessions.

1) An Understanding of Mindfulness Principles

It is important to clear up any misunderstandings that students may have gleaned from previous learning about mindfulness online. In particular, it is worth checking the use of apps and online videos that may have promoted 'relaxation and avoidance' or other approaches as being intrinsic mindfulness principles.

2) Digital Self-Awareness—Waking Up to the *Digital* Autopilot

It is important that students learn to develop an awareness of how digital interactions make them feel. This involves staying awake to the physical, emotional and psychological effects of digital interactions as they occur in the moment. This is similar to the regular 'waking up of the autopilot' approach used within mindfulness which involves reacquainting oneself with unconscious habits by becoming aware of underlying sensations. However, there are reasons why this may present particular challenges to new students. The actual physical and emotional experiences that accompany digital interactions may be difficult to access having been buried under years of habitual cognising that comes with computer use, i.e. it may be difficult to get beyond 'thinking' about digital interactions. This will require particular strategies. In addition, there is an important difference when considering the unconscious nature of the habits that are being unearthed. In the real world, unconsciousness refers to our reactions to situations that occur without conscious thought, e.g. when we rely on unconscious biases to make decisions about situations that are unhealthy or maladaptive. Digital unconsciousness may occur for the same reason, but it may also happen as a result of merging with digital 'extra-conscious' imperatives which are equally unhelpful but for different reasons. It is therefore important to become aware of the differences between unconscious and extra-conscious influences on immediate experience.

3) Techniques for Encouraging Digital Mindfulness

Suggestions have been offered here for dealing with the digital, hyper-real and algorithmic imperatives. In essence, they are all concerned with maintaining a persistent focus on the human imperative that recognises the personal and social impacts of using digital technologies.

Beyond Secular Mindfulness

Many of the experiences recounted in this book have addressed digital wellbeing in terms of bringing greater attention to the negative states that accompany digital interaction. This is perhaps unsurprising given that most participants came from an MBCT or MBSR background where mindfulness is designed to help those who are suffering psychologically. However, it seems that just treating mindfulness as a form of therapeutic attention training may not be sufficient to address the underlying compulsions that underpin digital interaction. It may be necessary to go back to some of the philosophical roots of mindfulness to really tackle the deeper issues at play. Buddhist and non-dualist approaches to meditation view mindfulness as a starting point for inquiring into the true nature of the self rather than an end in itself. Becoming aware of direct experience can provide an opportunity for questioning assumptions about the objective reality of the self and its relationship to thought. In the mindfulness of breathing practice, for instance: if you can give your full attention to the immediate experience of your breath, as you are breathing, you may find there comes a point where the self is no longer the central reference point—there is simply a direct 'experiencing' of the breath, without a thinker and in this, a sense of liberation from the self may be experienced. Likewise, 'thinking' about the experience also becomes redundant.

In digital scenarios, emphasis is placed on the interchange of thoughts enacted through keyboards and screens: it is inherently symbolic and this obscures direct experience as a means of self-transcendence. Whilst this study has shown that awareness of immediate physical sensations (such as breathing) can still be useful in maintaining attentional control, secular approaches to mindfulness do not usually make self-transcendence explicit as an aim. Typically, the approach seeks to develop detachment from (problematic) thought patterns, treating thoughts as transient events that are occurring without personal involvement, i.e. decentring (Kabat-Zinn, 1990; Williams & Penman, 2011). This process is implicitly self-transcendent (Garland & Fredrickson, 2019) but not always presented as such.

If self-transcendence is possible in digital scenarios, it must come through the compressed thought-action process that accompanies digital consumption and self-expression. In this context, the time between thought and action is so slight that we may need to slow our reactions down in order to bring awareness to the emotions and thoughts that present themselves whilst this is going on.

To give an example, you are probably reading this text through a screen and there are physical sensations related to you doing this. Consider for a moment the physical experience of your own breath or the way that light enters your eyes whilst you are reading. Notice whether you are holding your breath at all or whether there are places of tension in your body. Is it possible to notice this whole experience rather than just the thoughts that relate to the cognitive activity of reading? Now take a short break from the screen and see how this feels—revisiting those immediate physical sensations. Is it possible to be sensitive to the differences between your own thoughts and feelings as they are versus those provoked by the digital text?

Now consider a more dynamic experience of scrolling through social media posts or your emails—is it possible to observe this as a whole experience where you notice how it affects not only your thoughts, but your emotions and physical sensations as well? Is it possible to differentiate those reactions that are provoked by extra-conscious imperatives (the digital, algorithmic or hyper-real) from those that are uniquely due to your own human consciousness?

In order to thrive in a digital world, we must learn to be sensitive to the way in which digital interactions affect how we think and feel but we must also acknowledge a human inclination towards mindless states. Mindless or dissociative states are common experiences across humanity, present in reactions to trauma, experiences of hypnosis, trance states, hallucinogenic drugs, dreams, meditation, listening to music, television and all manner of digital interactions (Butler, 2004). These moments of 'no mind', where we exist without thought can move us beyond the limited sense of self that we experience in our everyday lives. They have potential as moments of insight, but they can also make us vulnerable to outside influence. Mindless states are not the opposite of mindfulness but merely the absence of conscious thought. As such, they can exist in many forms with some more beneficial than others. As the Zen Buddhist Suzuki (1970, p. 105) commented, "this 'no mind' is Zen mind which includes everything". What matters is bringing awareness to these moments and recognising what intercedes when there is an absence of thought. Unfortunately, what seems to happen with mindless states in digital environments is that these moments can be hijacked as opportunities for extra-conscious influence to assert itself. The challenge for digital approaches to mindfulness is to become aware of these mindless states as they are happening and to differentiate which are beneficial and which are not.

Limitations of This Study

The research in this book has allowed an investigation into how those engaged in mindfulness practice manage to integrate the digital world into their lives. Their experiences have revealed specific areas of concern with regard to mindless influence coming through digital design, commercial interests and the social norms of the internet. The book has gone some way towards defining a digital approach to mindfulness that will be of interest to Cyberpsychologists and mindfulness practitioners.

It should be remembered that this was based on a small study using qualitative interviews. As such, the findings may be difficult to generalise to other cohorts where age, cultural background or specific digital interests (e.g. gamers or those using dedicated work-based applications) have not been accounted for here. Having said that, the underlying principles of attention and unconscious bias that this study emphasises are universal.

Most of the participants had learnt about mindfulness through MBCT or MBSR courses and this meant that they were particularly focused on the therapeutic uses of mindfulness hence an emphasis on negative digital experiences. Mindfulness has a role to play in other more enjoyable and beneficial uses of digital devices that may not have been part of this analysis.

The COVID-19 Context

The specific historical context for this research is also important to note. The interviews were conducted during the global pandemic when everyday freedoms had been severely restricted and normal socialising and opportunities to meet others had been seriously curtailed. Countries who opted for such lockdowns saw digital screen time increase sharply (Sultana et al., 2021) as citizens became more reliant on digital forms of social and pragmatic support. Given this context, the participants of the study were likely to have been more dependent on their digital forms of contact and connection than they had been at any time before in their lives.

This prolonged situation had serious social and psychological implications. It increased experiences of social isolation and loneliness (Groarke et al., 2020) and exacerbated depression, anxiety and poor sleeping patterns (Khubchandani et al., 2021; Panchal et al., 2021; Pieh et al., 2021). During this period, social media served many functions, offering an important source of social contact (Cauberghe et al., 2021) but also distorting awareness of current affairs and creating conditions for information overload (Liu et al., 2021), disinformation (Nguyen & Catalan-Matamoros, 2020) and further amplification of unconscious tendencies (Buchanan et al., 2021).

Participants in this study will have likely seen any dysfunctional relationships with digital technology further amplified by the COVID-19 lockdowns and this is worth taking into account. Their use of mindfulness-based approaches became particularly relevant to the digital world at difficult moments during the pandemic and this was evident in some of the interviews. Whilst this provided a unique opportunity for studying digital mindfulness, it may not reflect their post-pandemic relationships with the same technologies. It did, however, reveal an extraordinary synthesis of digital and mindful ways of being that others would benefit from knowing about. It is likely that their involvement in mindfulness during this time will also have had a buffering effect on their psychological wellbeing during the pandemic (Widha et al., 2021).

References

Australian Government. (2021). *Online safety bill.* Department of communications, Urban infrastructure, Cities and the arts. https://www.legislation.gov.au/Details/C2021B00018

Bradley, S. D., Angelini, J. R., & Lee, S. (2007). Psychophysiological and memory effects of negative political ads: Aversive, arousing, and well remembered. *Journal of Advertising, 36*(4), 115–127.

Buchanan, K., Aknin, L. B., Lotun, S., & Sandstrom, G. M. (2021). Brief exposure to social media during the COVID-19 pandemic: Doom-scrolling has negative emotional consequences, but kindness-scrolling does not. *PLoS ONE, 16*(10), e0257728.

Butler, L. D. (2004). The Dissociations of Everyday Life. *Journal of Trauma & Dissociation, 5*(2), 1–11

Clark, A., & Chalmers, D. (1998). The Extended Mind. *Analysis, 58*(1), 7–19.

Cauberghe, V., Van Wesenbeeck, I., De Jans, S., Hudders, L., & Ponnet, K. (2021). How adolescents use social media to cope with feelings of loneliness and anxiety during COVID-19 lockdown. *Cyberpsychology, Behavior, and Social Networking, 24*(4), 250–257.

Dailey, S. L., Howard, K., Roming, S. M., Ceballos, N., & Grimes, T. (2020). A biopsychosocial approach to understanding social media addiction. *Human Behavior and Emerging Technologies, 2*(2), 158–167.

Elliott, A. (2019). *The culture of AI: Everyday life and the digital revolution.* Routledge.

European Commission. (2020). *Proposal for a regulation on a single market For digital services (Digital services act).* https://eur-lex.europa.eu/legal-content/en/TXT/?qid=1608117147218&uri=COM%3A2020%3A825%3AFIN

Freud, S. (1905). Three essays on the theory of sexuality. In J. Strachey (Ed.), *The standard edition of the complete psychological works of Sigmund Freud*, Vol. 7. Hogarth Press. Republished, 1956.

Garland, E. L., & Fredrickson, B. L. (2019). Positive psychological states in the arc from mindfulness to self-transcendence: Extensions of the Mindfulness-to-Meaning Theory and applications to addiction and chronic pain treatment. *Current Opinion in Psychology, 28*, 184–191.

Goldenberg, A., & Gross, J. J. (2020). Digital emotion contagion. *Trends in Cognitive Sciences, 24*(4), 316–328.

Groarke, J. M., Berry, E., Graham-Wisener, L., McKenna-Plumley, P. E., McGlinchey, E., & Armour, C. (2020). Loneliness in the UK during the COVID-19 pandemic: Cross-sectional results from the COVID-19 Psychological Wellbeing Study. *PLoS ONE, 15*(9), e0239698.

Hagey, K., & Horwitz, J. (2021). Facebook tried to make its platform a healthier place. It got angrier instead. *The Wall Street Journal, 16*.

Harley, D. (2019). The Link between Digital Disconnection and Death Anxiety: A Preliminary Study. *Annual Review of Cybertherapy and Telemedicine, 2019*, 115–120.

Kabat-Zinn, J. (1990). *Full catastrophe living: How to cope with stress, pain and illness using mindfulness meditation*. Bantam Dell.

Kardefelt-Winther, D. (2014). A conceptual and methodological critique of internet addiction research: Towards a model of compensatory internet use. *Computers in Human Behavior, 31*, 351–354.

Khubchandani, J., Sharma, S., Webb, F. J., Wiblishauser, M. J., & Bowman, S. L. (2021). Post-lockdown depression and anxiety in the USA during the COVID-19 pandemic. *Journal of Public Health, 43*(2), 246–253.

Kircaburun, K., Alhabash, S., Tosuntaş, ŞB., & Griffiths, M. D. (2020). Uses and gratifications of problematic social media use among university students: A simultaneous examination of the Big Five of personality traits, social media platforms, and social media use motives. *International Journal of Mental Health and Addiction, 18*(3), 525–547.

Kozyreva, A., Lorenz-Spreen, P., Hertwig, R., Lewandowsky, S., & Herzog, S. M. (2021). Public attitudes towards algorithmic personalization and use of personal data online: Evidence from Germany, Great Britain, and the United States. *Humanities and Social Sciences Communications, 8*(1), 1–11.

Lang, A., Park, B., Sanders-Jackson, A. N., Wilson, B. D., & Wang, Z. (2007). Cognition and emotion in TV message processing: How valence, arousing content, structural complexity and information density affect the availability of cognitive resources. *Media Psychology, 10*(3), 317–338.

Liu, H., Liu, W., Yoganathan, V., & Osburg, V. S. (2021). COVID-19 information overload and generation Z's social media discontinuance intention during the pandemic lockdown. *Technological Forecasting and Social Change, 166*, 120600.

McGilchrist, I. (2019). *The master and his emissary*. Yale University Press.

Nguyen, A., & Catalan-Matamoros, D. (2020). Digital mis/disinformation and public engagement with health and science controversies: Fresh perspectives from Covid-19. *Media and Communication, 8*(2), 323–328.

Oldenburg, R. (1999). *The Great Good Place: Cafés, Coffee Shops, Community Centers, Beauty Parlors, General Stores, Bars, Hangouts, and How They Get You Through The Day*. Marlowe & Company.

Panchal, U., Salazar de Pablo, G., Franco, M., Moreno, C., Parellada, M., Arango, C., & Fusar-Poli, P. (2021). The impact of COVID-19 lockdown on child and adolescent mental health: systematic review. *European child & adolescent psychiatry*, 1–27.

Park, C. S. (2015). Applying "negativity bias" to Twitter: Negative news on Twitter, emotions, and political learning. *Journal of Information Technology & Politics, 12*(4), 342–359.

Pieh, C., Budimir, S., Delgadillo, J., Barkham, M., Fontaine, J. R., & Probst, T. (2021). Mental health during COVID-19 lockdown in the United Kingdom. *Psychosomatic Medicine, 83*(4), 328–337.

Risko, E. F., & Gilbert, S. J. (2016). (2016) Cognitive offloading. *Trends in Cognitive Sciences, 20*(9), 676–688.

Sultana, A., Tasnim, S., Hossain, M. M., Bhattacharya, S., & Purohit, N. (2021). Digital screen time during the COVID-19 pandemic: A public health concern. *F1000Research, 10*(81), 81.

Suzuki, S. (1970). *Zen mind, beginner's mind*. Weatherhill.

Trengove, M., Kazim, E., RS Almeida, D., Hilliard, A., Lomas, E., & Zannone, S. (2022, April 1). *A digital duty of care: A critical review of the online safety bill*.

UK Government. (2021). *Draft online safety bill*. Department of Digital, Culture, Media, and Sport. https://assets.publishing.service.gov.uk/government/uploads/system/uploads/attachment_data/file/985033/Draft_Online_Safety_Bill_Bookmarked.pdf

Wang, Q., Lee, D., & Hou, Y. (2017). Externalising the autobiographical self: Sharing personal memories online facilitated memory retention. *Memory, 25*, 772–776.

Wells, G., Horwitz, J., & Seetharaman, D. (2021). Facebook knows Instagram is toxic for teen girls, company documents show. *The Wall Street Journal*.

Widha, L., Rahmat, H. K., & Basri, A. S. H. (2021, March). A review of mindfulness therapy to improve psychological well-being during the COVID-19 pandemic. In *Proceeding International Conference on Science and Engineering*, Vol. 4, 383–386.

Williams, M., & Penman, D. (2011). *Mindfulness: a practical guide to finding peace in a frantic world*. Hachette UK.

Zuboff, S. (2019). *The age of surveillance capitalism: The fight for a human future at the new frontier of power*. Public Affairs.

Index

A

advertising 10, 15, 83–84
algorithms 15–16, 58–64, 68, 78–80, 82–92
anchoring 71–72, 81
anxiety 3, 6, 13, 27, 30, 31, 34, 44, 52, 56–58, 63, 67, 69, 78, 81, 87, 93
attention 9–16, 66, 68, 70, 72, 78–93
   information processing model of 12
   selective 13–14
attentional bias 14–16, 84
attentional capacity 27, 34, 57, 78
attentional control 28, 31, 32, 34
   delegation of 78, 84
attention economy 15, 87

B

being mode 30
Buddhism 26–27, 72, 90–92
   and the noble eight fold path 26
   Zen 48, 91–92

C

cognitive-motor dual task interference 57
cognitive outsourcing 79
compassion 72
compulsive use 61–62, 86
coping 29, 31, 86
   maladaptive 31
   strategies 30, 31
Coronavirus/Covid-19 Pandemic 2, 93

D

deautomatization 31
decentring 30, 91
depression 5, 9, 27, 30, 31, 34, 52, 62, 93
digital
　addiction 7–9
　dependency 2–16, 31, 44, 86
　design 10, 15–16, 33, 64, 90, 92
　detox 44
　disconnection 67–68
　habits 30–35
　imperative 30–35
　mindfulness 53, 66–73, 90
　rumination 61–62, 65, 66, 79, 84
　self-awareness 49–65
　wellbeing 2–16, 90
displacement 3–10
　as a defence mechanism 10
　of attention 2, 58, 86
　of healthy behaviour 2
　of social activity 9
dissociation 60
doing mode 30
'do Not Disturb' mode 68
doomscrolling 34
dopamine release 8

H

hermeneutic phenomenology 48
hyper-reality 84–86
hyper-social dilemmas 63–65

I

identity play 6
information overload 61, 78, 93

internet vii, viii, 2–5, 7–9, 11, 14, 15, 33, 50, 51, 57, 58, 82–86, 92
　addiction 7–10
　penetration 2
interruptions 13

M

mindfulness
　apps 53
　as a trait 34
　as Buddhist practice 26–28
　as distraction preventer 35
　as pain relief 27
　as regular practice 51
　as self-help 52
　as therapeutic practice 33–35
　misunderstandings of 49–52
mindfulness-based cognitive therapy (MBCT) 27–34, 51, 52, 55, 68, 90, 93
mindfulness-based stress reduction (MBSR) 27–34, 51, 52, 55, 68, 90, 93
mindfulness 14–15, 26–35, 60, 86
multitasking 12–13, 57, 58, 78, 81–82

N

nomophobia 6
non-dualism 90

O

overthinking 61–62

GPSR Compliance
The European Union's (EU) General Product Safety Regulation (GPSR) is a set
of rules that requires consumer products to be safe and our obligations to
ensure this.

If you have any concerns about our products, you can contact us on

ProductSafety@springernature.com

In case Publisher is established outside the EU, the EU authorized
representative is:

Springer Nature Customer Service Center GmbH
Europaplatz 3
69115 Heidelberg, Germany

www.ingramcontent.com/pod-product-compliance
Ingram Content Group UK Ltd.
Pitfield, Milton Keynes, MK11 3LW, UK
UKHW021251180426

11946UKWH00004B/86